40 Great Flight Simulator Adventures

Charles Gulick

COMPUTE! Publications,Inc. **abc**
One of the ABC Publishing Companies
Greensboro, North Carolina

Printed in the United States of America

10 9 8 7 6 5 4 3 2

ISBN 0-87455-022-X

COMPUTE! Publications, Inc., Post Office Box 5406, Greensboro, NC 27403, (919) 275-9809, is one of the ABC Publishing Companies and is not associated with any manufacturer of personal computers. Commodore 64 is a trademark of Commodore Electronics Limited. Apple II is a trademark of Apple Computer, Inc. Atari is a trademark of Atari, Inc. IBM PC and PCjr are trademarks of International Business Machines, Inc.

Flight Simulator is produced by Microsoft Corporation and copyright 1984 by Bruce Artwick. *Flight Simulator II* is produced by SubLogic Corporation and copyright 1984 by Bruce Artwick.

Contents

Foreword

Bruce Artwick's first version of *Flight Simulator* was released in 1979 and ran on the Apple II with just 16K of memory. Since then, *Flight Simulator* for the IBM PC and PCjr and *Flight Simulator II* for Apple, Atari, and Commodore 64 personal computers have become huge successes. These second-generation simulations added more color, 3-D graphics, and more-realistic flying.

Thousands of computer users have enjoyed the experience of flight with these programs. And now, with COMPUTE!'s *40 Great Flight Simulator Adventures*, both experienced aviators and rookie pilots can enjoy the thrill and excitement of flying 40 customized flight simulator scenarios.

Each scenario takes you on a tour through the air, and puts an instructor and guide right beside you. Parameters are provided to position your aircraft in midflight or on the ground waiting for takeoff. The realism of *Flight Simulator* and *Flight Simulator II*—so realistic that the controls may seem intimidating at first—is turned to your advantage in each scenario. With clear directions and thorough advice, *40 Great Flight Simulator Adventures* gently takes you from the ground to the stratosphere.

Imagine yourself in the cockpit of your Piper 181 Cherokee Archer, flying over mountains, around skyscrapers, and between the twin towers of the World Trade Center. Experience the danger of night flying, soaring upside down, or landing your airplane without any power.

Can you save the golden-haired girl on Catalina Island? The weather is terrible and no other pilot will risk it. You can't use your radar and you'll have to make a touchdown with just your instruments.

Or maybe you'd prefer a pleasant flight along the Kankakee River or an aerial tour of New York City.

You'll even see sights undocumented in the manuals, like a mysterious airport (is it a secret base?) and strange aerial phenomena (have you entered the Twilight Zone?).

With your copy of *Flight Simulator* or *Flight Simulator II*, a computer, and this book, you can experience all these and more. With *40 Great Flight Simulator Adventures* as your instructor and guide, you'll learn tricks and maneuvers you never imagined possible.

Introduction and Instructions

Welcome aboard. And take the left seat.

The adventures I invite you to share here are designed to enhance your enjoyment of *Flight Simulator* and *Flight Simulator II* by introducing some of their limitless possibilities, beauties, and challenges. To me, designer Bruce Artwick's programs are brilliant achievements, works conceived and executed with bravura and great genius.

Not Text—the Voice of the Flight Instructor

This is not a book to be *read* in the usual sense, but to be kept open across your knees or on your flight desk while you're flying. Once you have become familiar with the operation of the simulator as described in the manuals that come with the program, you are ready to fly the adventures in this book.

To experience an adventure, you must first set up its parameters in the edit mode, using a custom mode number. There are elements of suspense, surprise, and mystery in addition to navigation, communication, and other advisories. These are meaningful only if you're flying while you read and vice versa. Think of the text as the voice of a flight instructor, a local guide, or simply a friend along for the ride.

Don't expect to fly all adventures flawlessly the first or even the fiftieth time, even if you're skilled at flying the simulator. Interfacing the text and operations requires both familiarization and practice. And if we were able to fly perfectly, who'd want to? Even the eagle is always learning.

Setting Up Adventure Modes

With the simulator loaded, press Esc (E on the Commodore 64) to enter edit mode. At the top of your screen, under "Simulation Control," you'll see "User mode," and an arrow pointing to the number of the mode you're currently in. It should be 0 if you just loaded the simulator.

If you're not at User mode 0, type and enter a 0 to get there.

Next, change the User mode number to the next available mode starting with 10 and numbering to 24 (29 on an IBM). For instance, in the first adventure, "Low Pass on the Pacific," change the mode number to 10. This is done by entering a value of 100 plus the desired number, in our example the value 110. Type 110 and press RETURN or Enter. You'll see the User mode number change to 10. (If you type a mode number without adding 100, all parameters will switch to spurious values which must be corrected—a lot of unnecessary typing.)

Should you wish to change the Sound, Autocoordination, or Communication rate parameters, advance the arrow and do so. But this book assumes you're flying with Reality 0 (off) and the control parameters as they are found at the preset User mode 0. (You can, if you want, set a different communication rate.)

Now change each parameter under "Aircraft Position"— North position, East position, Altitude, and so forth—as given at the pertinent adventure heading. Then do the same under the "Environmental" heading. Change only those values which are listed for the adventure. Leave Cloud layers at 0 unless the chapter calls for other values. Note that "Wind" in this book refers to Surface wind. Be sure to set both velocity (knots) and direction (degrees). Except for a few adventures, winds aloft and shear altitudes remain as you find them in preset mode 0.

Check your entries very carefully. A wrong or omitted digit could radically change the result of an adventure.

When you have entered and checked all parameters, press the appropriate key to save the current mode to the mode library (Ins for IBM; S on Apples and the Commodore 64; CTRL-S for Atari). The mode you have set up is now saved until you turn off the computer. (See below for saving modes permanently to disk.)

Follow the procedure above to set up any and all of the custom modes in this book. You may enter the parameters of 15 (20 on the IBM) of this book's 40 custom modes while in edit mode. Or just type in 1 or 2 if you're eager to get started, then come back for the others later.

Adventure Tips. Before you press Esc (E on the Commodore 64) to exit edit mode, read the first line or so of the relevant chapter so that you'll know something about what to expect. Then exit and begin the adventure. Use the Pause (P) key as frequently as you like to catch up with or anticipate the text.

Make a habit of checking the heading on your instrument panel the moment you exit edit mode and confirm that it agrees with the heading called for at the start of the adventure (allow a second or two for the simulator to settle down). If the heading is not correct, press the reset (called Recall on the IBM) simulator key (PrtSc on the PC; Del on the PCjr; = on the Atari; + on the Commodore 64; SHIFT-+ on Apples). A one-degree difference should be ignored. But very often the simulator is far from the heading set up in edit mode, and you won't see what the text indicates you should, either on your panel or out your windshield.

Sometimes there will be other disparities, such as the wrong altitude. A wrong altitude will usually cause the aircraft to dive and crash. This has nothing to do with the parameters of the chapters (if you entered them correctly), but is one of several simulator phenomena. Only one adventure, "Another Fine Mess," deliberately begins with a form of crash, for reasons which will be made obvious. In no other adventure should the first thing you experience be a crash or splash or abnormally hairy attitude.

So whenever things don't seem right, use the reset (Recall on IBM) simulator key until what you're seeing agrees with what you're reading. (When you've flown an adventure a few times, you'll know immediately if the simulator's being ornery.)

This book is not a replacement for the manuals that came with the program. Although it is not necessary to know every detail in the manuals, you should be familiar with the basic controls and necessary keypresses of the simulator.

Flying a Mode

If you've just finished entering all parameters correctly, exit edit mode by pressing Esc (E on the Commodore 64). If you're switching from an old mode to a new one, position the arrow opposite User mode and enter the desired mode number. Then press the RETURN or Enter key (you'll see the parameters re-set to those of the selected mode), and exit the flight. If you are using an Atari you'll have to insert the Scenery disk to fly most of the adventures.

Sometimes the reset simulator key must be pressed several times before the simulator corrects itself to the true editor parameters. Make a habit of checking the heading, in particular, when you start a flight, to be sure it agrees with the editor.

It's important to fly all modes in this book with gear down, as if the gear were nonretractable. Speeds and many other parameters are based on that flight condition.

Three cues are provided to help you follow flight events:

 indicates the point where you're to take over the controls and fly the plane. Don't touch the controls until then.

 calls your attention to a view you should observe out your windshield or on radar. (Note that colors described will vary depending on the computer and the type of monitor or TV you're using.)

 signals that an action of some sort is required of you.

The 40 flights presented in the book will occupy three disks (two on the IBM). It's suggested that you enter and save the parameters for all 40 flights that appear in the book, placing the maximum number of flights on each disk (20 on each IBM disk and 15 for all other machines). I suggest you write the mode number and disk name in this book below the title of each adventure. That way you can readily find the parameters for any flight to which you want to return. As described in the *Flight Simulator* and *Flight Simulator II* manuals, modes 0 through 9 are preset modes and modes 10 to 24 (29 on an IBM) are User modes.

Resetting a Mode

While flying you can always reestablish a mode (return to the startup condition) by pressing the reset (Recall on IBM) simulator key (PrtSc on the PC; Del on the PCjr; = on the Atari; + on the Commodore 64; SHIFT-+ on Apples). This is useful if you've lost your way in regard to the instructions of a particular flight adventure or if you just want to start again.

Pressing the reset simulator key while in edit mode will also reset a mode to its original parameters. It's a good idea to do this every time you enter the edit mode to change modes, and necessary if you intend saving the mode to disk. Otherwise, parameters will be those in effect when you entered edit mode (for instance in midflight) rather than those of startup.

Saving Resident Modes to Disk

Enter edit mode. Remove the *Flight Simulator* disk and insert a blank disk. It need not be formatted. Press the appropriate key (S for the IBM; CTRL-Z for a Commodore 64, Apple, or Atari) to save the modes currently stored in the mode library. When you see the "Modes Saved" message or when your disk drive stops spinning, remove, label, and store the newly recorded disk until you wish to use it. If you wish to continue flying, reinsert the *Flight Simulator* disk and proceed as usual. *Remember to use a write-protect tab for permanent protection; saving to disk destroys all previous material on that disk.*

Loading a Custom Disk

Enter edit mode. Remove the *Flight Simulator* disk and insert the custom disk. Press the appropriate key to load (L for the

IBM; CTRL-X for the Commodore 64, Apple, and Atari). When you see the "Modes Loaded" message or when your disk drive stops spinning, remove the custom disk and reinsert the *Flight Simulator* disk. Press any key and proceed as usual.

It is my hope that this book will help you share the intense interest, excitement of discovery, and sheer fun I've had exploring Bruce Artwick's achievement.

Now I'm right here in the right seat. Let's get flying.

Charles Gulick
August, 1985

The
Adventures

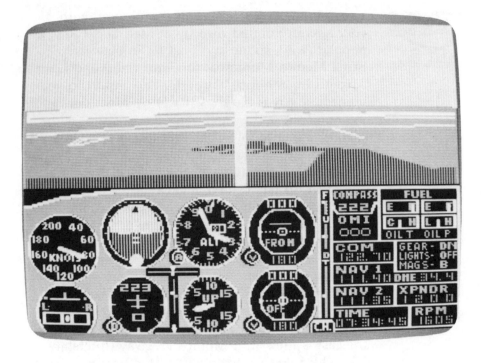

Low Pass on the Pacific

North Position: 15393
East Position: 5806
Altitude: 1220
Pitch: 358
Bank: 0
Heading: 223
Airspeed: 81
Throttle: 9760

Rudder: 32767
Ailerons: 32767
Flaps: 0
Elevators: 39935
Time: 7:30
Season: 2—Spring
Wind: 5 Kts, 180

You're in a gentle glide to the southwest, with your aircraft pointed directly at Marina del Rey, a popular (wild, some say) boat basin between Santa Monica Municipal (on your right) and Los Angeles International airports. The airport to your immediate left is Hughes (PVT). A zoom-out radar view will show the three airports as you near the marina. Santa Monica Bay and the Pacific Ocean stretch in the sunlight ahead.

You'll pass directly over the marina at about 1000 feet, so you'll have a close-up view. Sit back and enjoy. Your aircraft is in slow, but stable, flight. (That little white spot slipping off your screen to the left is, exactly, nothing. Take my word. I checked it out.)

When you're past the harbor and can see only the inlet and ocean, take a rear view. The north-south highway behind you is the San Diego Free-way (Interstate 405), and the road cutting in from the east is the Santa Monica Freeway (Interstate 10), which you could follow all the way to Jacksonville, Florida—if you had enough gas. In the background are the San Gabriel Mountains, about 20 miles away. Keep the rear view until you get a look at the marina from the ocean side, slipping away under your tail.

Now switch to a left rear view and take a low altitude glance at Los Angeles International Airport, behind you across the inlet. A right rear view will show you Santa Monica as it might look on the downwind leg of a landing approach.

Next look directly behind you again and see it all—a fine panorama of the shoreline, Marina del Rey, the San Gabriel Mountains, and finally a bit of Los Angeles International. Don't touch the controls until you have that whole picture. You're losing very little if any altitude, probably have between 700 and 1000 feet, and the Pacific is, of course, at sea level. So enjoy the view fully before you take over.

 Now add power to get an rpm reading of 2000. While climbing, tune your NAV to the Santa Catalina VOR, 111.4, and get a heading. Then fly to that swank little island's airport, about 35 miles south. Tower is 122.7, elevation 1602. There you can fish, swim on some beautiful natural beaches, play tennis, or go horseback riding. William Wrigley, Jr., had his home on Catalina, and invested some of the fortune he made (selling chewing gum) to bring art and culture to the island. You can still find some of the chewing gum there, stuck under the seats in the movie theater.

Dead-Stick off
San Clemente

North Position: 14974
East Position: 5664
Altitude: 5000
Pitch: 0
Bank: 0
Heading: 245
Airspeed: 122
Throttle: 0

Rudder: 32767
Ailerons: 32767
Flaps: 0
Elevators: 32767
Time: 16:00
Season: 3—Summer
Wind: 16 Kts, 230

Please read the entire text before beginning this flight.

 You're straight and level at 5000 feet when your engine quits. (It quit the instant you exited edit mode, as simulated by Throttle 0. You may *not* use throttle from here on out.)

You must make a dead-stick landing on San Clemente Island, which is directly below you.

Though your Los Angeles chart shows the island almost due south of Catalina, it doesn't show the terrain. Neither does it show (nor does the simulator) that there is, in the real world, a navy runway across the northern end of San Clemente. This runway appears on the FAA Los Angeles sectional chart.

If you can make it to the runway, your chances of a respectable landing (though the navy won't be cheering) are excellent. Its elevation is about 20 feet above sea level.

Your second best choice is to land somewhere along the relatively flat western side of the island. The rocky eastern side presents an engraved invitation to disaster.

Will you attempt the navy runway? And if so, from which direction? (Assume the navy runway numbers are 5/23.) Or will you settle for somewhere along the west shore? Of course, you might very well survive a ditch attempt, too, but it'd be a lonely swim.

Rate yourself an expert if you land safely on the northern tip of the island and on a heading of 230. The closer you are to the water (short of a splash!), the better. (You're not close enough to the water to say you've landed on the tip of the island, from either direction, unless you can see the northeast or southwest corners of the geography out your windshield.) If you land on the northern tip heading anywhere from 220 to 240, though not 230 exactly, you're still superpilot. Otherwise, for your approach from the east, don't feel too smug even if you set her down safely.

For a landing on the same end of the island, but from the opposite direction—and on a heading of 50 degrees—rate yourself a semiexpert, with appropriate reservations as above for up to 10-degree deviations from the runway heading, and for the picture out your windshield.

For a landing anywhere on the west shore, consider yourself an advanced fledgling. And for any other kind of landing anywhere else on the island (not involving a crash, of course), think of yourself as at least "a pilot," since there's a chance you'd walk away from it.

Finally, unless you're serious when you say you can walk on water, give yourself a zero for any blue Pacific conclusion.

A crash will automatically put you in a new try. But crash or not, practice may eventually get you that coveted "Hey, who are you?" from the navy San Clemente tower.

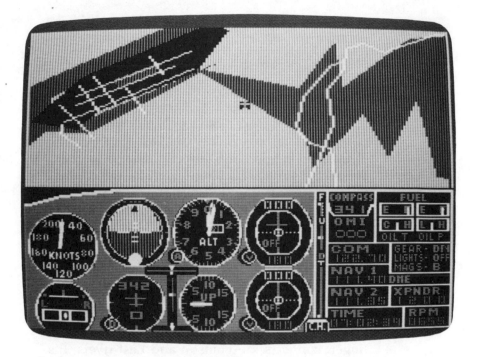

To Breathe Free

North Position: 17097
East Position: 21028
Altitude: 22
Pitch: 0
Bank: 0
Heading: 240
Airspeed: 0
Throttle: 0

Rudder: 32767
Ailerons: 32767
Flaps: 0
Elevators: 32767
Time: 7:00
Season: 2—Spring
Wind: 3 Kts, 206

You've turned onto runway 22 at New York's La Guardia Airport, ready to taxi into position for takeoff.

But first, use radar to examine your location. Zoom out until the runway disappears. You'll see three separate bodies of water, two of which, at about two o'clock, join like a pair of needle-points. The thinner one is the East River, and the arrowhead-shaped one, directly behind you, is Flushing Bay. The bay joins with Long Island Sound just past the Bronx-Whitestone and Throgs Neck bridges, visible with their connecting high-ways on your screen. The broad blue brush stroke is the Hudson River. The geography to your right (this side of the Hudson) is the south end of the Bronx, and to your left, the Borough of Queens.

Zoom out one more notch. The pointing finger is Manhattan. A little sluiceway of water that doesn't show, but is about at the knuckle of the finger, connects the Hudson and East rivers. It's what makes Manhattan an island.

Return to your out-the-windshield view. The three buildings in the distance are the Empire State Building and the twin 110-floor World Trade Center towers. Just beyond the latter, but invisible at your elevation, is the Statue of Liberty. We're going to see all three from the air.

Take off and climb straight out. Plan to level off at 1500, but as you pass through 750, start a shallow right turn to head approximately west, or until the World Trade Center towers are positioned well to the left on your windshield. Your objective is to fly between the towers and the venerable Empire State Building, once the tallest building in the world, which is or shortly will be visible. Head your aircraft to achieve that.

Pause (P) before you fly too far, and admire the whole view below and ahead. You can see the East River (with the Manhattan Bridge to Brooklyn at the extreme left), all of downtown Manhattan, the Statue of Liberty (presently just a dot to the left of the Trade Center towers), and the Hudson River from its mouth in Upper Bay. If you have a bridge at the lower right on your windshield, that's the Queensboro Bridge. Across the Hudson is, of course, New Jersey. What doesn't show, here or in the simulation, are the beautiful steep cliffs—the Palisades—on the New Jersey side.

As you fly on, use your right and left side views to see first the Empire State Building, then the imposing World Trade Center. Finally, use a rear view to take in the whole area from the New Jersey side of the Hudson. Keep this view until the Statue of Liberty, still just a dot, comes into the scene on this side of the Hudson (far right on the screen when looking directly rear). We'll have a closer look at the lady.

Add carb heat, chop your power, and start a descent to an altitude of 500 feet. As you descend, do a fairly steep 180 (approximately) to the left, straightening out to get the statue directly ahead of your aircraft.

Continue your descent, if necessary, to get straight and level at 500. Slow-fly the airplane. And don't use Pause until after the simulator accesses its disk. The dot will transform into a full-figure statue, proud and solitary on its island. Get up close and personal. Time now to pause.

And reflect.

Once past the statue, climb to 1500 feet while setting up a course to the right of the Trade Center towers (if you're not already on same). You'll soon see La Guardia directly ahead. The winds haven't shifted, so over the East River turn left to head 40 degrees and you'll be downwind in a righthand pattern for runway 22.

 As the airport passes on your right, take the highest radar view that shows the intersecting strips. It's a great graphic.

 Then, about as the airport disappears off the bottom of your radar screen, return to out-the-windshield and turn base (130 degrees) for runway 22.

Enjoy your finale over Flushing Bay, too, where the runway reaches right to the edge of the water. For a while, at least, you've been far above the huddled masses that make New York the savage and beautiful place it is.

A Game of
Bridge

North Position: 17058
East Position: 20995
Altitude: 76
Pitch: 358
Bank: 0
Heading: 250
Airspeed: 81
Throttle: 9760

Rudder: 32767
Ailerons: 32767
Flaps: 0
Elevators: 40959
Time: 9:00
Season: 2—Spring
Wind: 10 Kts, 270

At times the simulator simply will not accept this mode, and the plane will crash due to a rapid drop in airspeed. However, the parameters are correct for a safe flight as described. If you experience repeated failures, I'd suggest you try another adventure, and then try this one again later. Sometimes, just a moment or so in Adventure 12, for example, makes this mode work properly.

You are at a hairy altitude in slow flight over the East River, just where it bends west under Manhattan Bridge. The southern extremity of Manhattan is on your right and Brooklyn is on your left. The people in all the buildings have come to their windows at the sound of your throttled-back engine. The people in the streets have all stopped to watch, too, wondering if you're going to buy it (and I don't mean purchase it). The phones are also ringing off the hook in every police precinct in the area.

Because, yes, you're going to fly—or try to fly—between the superstructure and the roadway of Manhattan Bridge, passing just to the right of the center pier. You've only a few feet to spare.

The chances are excellent if you don't touch the controls, because you're pretty stable just as you are. Sit this first one out and watch. The actual fly-through happens pretty fast, because Manhattan Bridge is, after all, only a road's width on the landscape.

 Relive this adventure a few times using reset (Recall on IBM).

 Take different views each time you make the pass to see the event from several angles. Try a radar close-up, too. And if you have any doubts that you're actually just above the traffic level, take a straight-down view and see the bridge go by under you.

 After a few passes, take the controls and try some variations. Maybe fly under some sections. Maybe over at other points. You can try anything once.

But sometimes, in the real world, *only* once.

A Sound Approach

North Position: 17606
East Position: 22132
Altitude: 4468
Pitch: 0
Bank: 0
Heading: 238
Airspeed: 126
Throttle: 22000 (IBM only)
Throttle: 19952 (all except IBM)

Rudder: 32767
Ailerons: 32767
Flaps: 0
Elevators: 33023 (IBM only)
Elevators: 37119 (all except IBM)
Time: 16:44
Season: 3—Summer
Wind: 15 Kts, 180

Approximately 20 nautical miles ahead of you is Martha's Vineyard, a resort island off the southern coast of Massachusetts. You're about 55 miles southeast of Boston.

 Access radar and adjust your zoom until you see the mainland and two somewhat triangular islands. The section of mainland you're over is Cape Cod, itself an island by virtue of a canal which divides it from the spherical land mass on your right. The body of water there and behind you is Cape Cod Bay.

The triangular island to the left is Nantucket, where, sad to say, elegant museums and artifacts commemorate sea captains who amassed great wealth hunting and killing whales. The water you're over now is Nantucket Sound. Go to the out-the-windshield view.

Tune NAV 2 to Martha's Vineyard VOR, 108.2, and you'll find you're on or close to the 240-degree radial. Tune NAV 1 to the Martha's Vineyard ILS (Instrument Landing System) frequency, 108.7, and set the OBI to 240 with a TO indication. Fly that needle to get on the 240 radial.

When your DME reads 17 to 18 nautical miles, you'll see the Martha's Vineyard airport straight ahead. You're on a long final for runway 24.

The objectives here, besides sightseeing, are to practice setting up a pattern approach speed and tracking the glideslope needle.

This long approach gives you a chance to experiment and familiarize yourself with glidepath vagaries. The horizontal needle represents the desired glideslope. Don't sweat it, however, until it moves toward the center of the instrument. Then it's ready to work.

Reduce power and set up your approach. Use flaps or not to suit yourself.

Adjust pitch to get and keep the glideslope needle centered. And use power to maintain the desired airspeed. Or use them in any combination that you've learned or that suits you. Meanwhile, keep the vertical needle centered.

That sounds so simple, doesn't it?

But if you're new to this sort of thing, you'll find your eyes are glued to the instruments (note plural). You'll think there must be an awful lot of turbulence or something up here.

When the glideslope needle goes below the centerline—as it surely will—give down elevator and/or reduce power. When the needle goes above the line—as it just as surely will, often— give up elevator and/or.... But keep everlastingly at it. Get on top of it. Anticipate. Coax. Fight. Encourage. Fly the thing. Don't let it fly you.

Just as everlastingly, try to maintain your approach speed. Your eyes will dance (through the glue) from the airspeed indicator to the glideslope needle, and back and forth, and you may get into some wild attitude and airspeed configurations, depending on your experience. It's a charming and challenging game.

And don't forget to keep lined up with the runway. (At least you have visual contact on this flight, for which be thankful, but if you're inspired, use just the ILS vertical needle, which indicates the runway centerline.) Listen for the outer marker signal. And slow to landing speed for the flare.

This is a neat way to spend a Sunday afternoon, particularly if it's raining outside (real world). But at some time or another, it says here, persistence is supposed to win. Probably when you least expect it, you'll find you've very prettily set her down—and right on the money. So when you feel you have the hang of it, add some clouds with bottoms around 250 feet (field elevation is 68 feet) and fly the ILS for real.

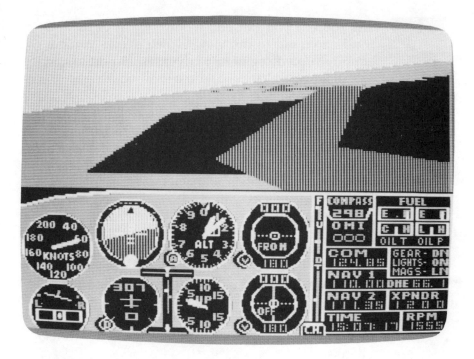

Fly Me a River

North Position: 16862
East Position: 16625
Altitude: 1000
Pitch: 359
Bank: 0
Heading: 226
Airspeed: 74
Throttle: 10724

Rudder: 32767
Ailerons: 32767
Flaps: 0
Elevators: 41216
Time: 15:00
Season: 3—Summer
Wind: 4 Kts, 160

21

As soon as you exit edit mode, switch in radar and zoom out to the view, which shows you an uninterrupted segment of river, an airport ahead at about one o'clock, and a city to your right.

Press P once you have this radar view so that you can get acquainted with the surroundings.

You're flying over the Kankakee River in Illinois, at a point about 30 miles south of Chicago. The airport on your radar screen is Greater Kankakee and the city you see is (as you've probably guessed) Kankakee.

Now resume your flight and your out-the-windshield view. Retain the slow-flight mode and maintain 1000 feet as you fly the meandering course of the river. Try to time and execute your turns so that you're always in harmony with the natural flow of the river and always between its banks.

The effect may be for you, as it was for me, a pleasant and gentle one. And you may experience, particularly as you approach the point where the river bends through the city, some of the calm and serenity that a river lends to a landscape and to our sensibilities.

Each turn provides a new horizon for the eye and, by the same chemistry, for the mind. Perhaps you'll feel, as I did, that this is a river you'll return to sometimes. Just to fly it. To see where its vistas might take the imagination. Or for the soothing effects of distance—the feeling of space somehow separate from time.

How far does this river go, you might wonder, as I did the first time I flew it. And one thing I knew for certain: I wouldn't stop until I reached the end. The river was like a narrative I had to finish.

On Kankakee, each curve of the blue on the landscape leads to another. I was reminded of the allegory of a boat traveling a winding river. An observer standing on a section of riverbank the boat has passed can no longer see it, thus, it's in the past to him, just as his presence there is an event of the past to the occupants of the boat. Meanwhile, a pilot in a plane above sees the observer on the riverbank plus the boat and everything its occupants observe. Further, the pilot sees what is around the next bend of the river, which for the boaters is the future. So, past, present, and future for everyone below is just a single moment for the seer with the wings.

As a suggestion, why not do a 180 when you reach the end and see the river from the opposite perspective?

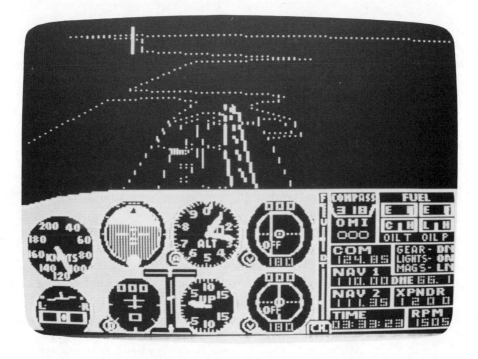

Midnight Ride

North Position: 17155
East Position: 16675
Altitude: 2362
Pitch: 359
Bank: 0
Heading: 352
Airspeed: 80
Throttle: 10500

Rudder: 32767
Ailerons: 32767
Flaps: 0
Elevators: 39935
Time: 3:30
Season: 1—Winter
Wind: 8 Kts, 90

You're at or around approach speed and configuration, inbound to Meigs (where were you until 3:30 a.m., anyway?). You're cleared for a straight-in approach to runway 36.

 Take over and continue, making any and all corrections to suit your purpose and your flying preferences.

The purpose here is to give you a readily accessible setup for practicing approaches and landings in general and night approaches and landings in particular.

The most useful technique for such practice, I find, is to deliberately vary your configuration so that you're not always approaching in the same familiar one. That means vary both your heading and your altitude along with power setting if desired.

For example, once you depart the edit mode, you might climb a couple of hundred feet higher and then take up the approach. Or turn to a heading 15 or 20 degrees to the left or right of the one provided, and then settle down to your approach and landing.

Another variation might be to assume your landing is from the opposite direction; in other words, you are cleared to land on runway 18 rather than 36. Either direction, it's a crosswind landing.

In any event, considering the hour, I trust you are sober and are concentrated solely upon flying the airplane. Should you feel drowsy, pull over to the curb and shut down the engine.

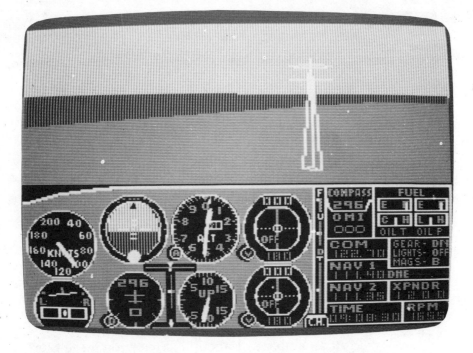

Threading the Needle

North Position: 21344
East Position: 6611
Altitude: 30
Pitch: 0
Bank: 0
Heading: 293
Airspeed: 0
Throttle: 0

Rudder: 32767
Ailerons: 32767
Flaps: 0
Elevators: 32767
Time: 9:00
Season: 2—Spring
Wind: 7 Kts, 4

You're ready to taxi into position for runway 33 at Renton Municipal in Seattle.

Switch in your radar and zoom out until you see portions of three bodies of water on your screen.

To your left is Puget Sound, with Henry M. Jackson (Seattle-Tacoma) International Airport on its eastern bank. A bit north on the same highway, Interstate 5, is Boeing Field (King County) International. The water you'll take off over is Lake Washington, and the highway running alongside it is Interstate 405. Interstate 90 sweeps in from the east, and the little lake just to the right of it is Lake Sammamish.

We'll be flying contact at 1000 feet, so get lined up heading 330 degrees and take off when you're ready. Use a shallow climbout so that you'll be able to see the landscape over your nose.

At an altitude of about 500 feet, you'll see Mercer Island straight ahead. Hold your heading and continue your climb.

As you're leveling off at 1000 feet, turn left to a heading of about 300 degrees. You'll see some tall buildings out your windshield. Point toward the center of the cluster of them. Shortly, the simulator will access its disk, twice in the space of a few minutes. Then a single tower will stand forth—the Space Needle at Seattle Center.

Head straight toward the building and plan to fly over it at about 1000 feet. As you get closer, you'll see what looks like an observation tower at the top. This is a revolving restaurant, which offers a beautiful panoramic view of Seattle, Puget Sound, Mount Rainier, and, directly below, for the diners in the restaurant, other features preserved, like the Space Needle itself from the 1962 World's Fair.

The moment the Space Needle disappears under your nose, take a straight-down view. You'll get a dramatic close-up of the circular restaurant passing below you. Then set a direct rear view and see it recede off your tail, with Mount Rainier in the background.

When you're well out over Puget Sound, do a 180 and have another pass at the Space Needle.

The southernmost highway crossing Lake Washington, and intersecting Mercer Island, is I-90, ahead of you. When you can spot the runway at Renton, get into configuration to set down again on runway 33.

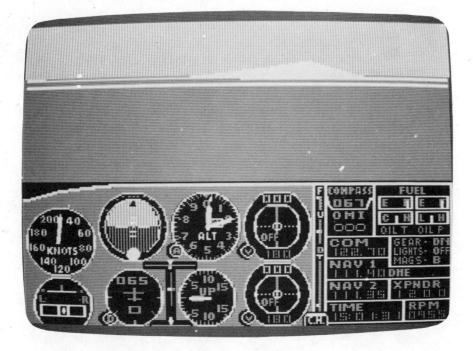

Tell It on the Mountain

North Position: 21219
East Position: 6339
Altitude: 204
Pitch: 0
Bank: 0
Heading: 90
Airspeed: 0
Throttle: 0

Rudder: 32767
Ailerons: 32767
Flaps: 0
Elevators: 32767
Time: 15:00
Season: 2—Spring
Wind: 5 Kts, 90

Get lined up for runway 8 here at Olympia Municipal (the city of Olympia is Washington's state capital, a staggering fact of which I had no inkling, did you?).

You'll see that you're also lined up for Mount Rainier, the highest point in the state—14,410 feet in the clouds.

You can fly to this majestic landmark visually, of course. But tune your NAV to Olympia VORTAC anyway (113.4) so that the DME, once we get to Rainier, will tell us just how far it is from where we're sitting now.

Take off, point for the peak, and just climb. And keep climbing. Full power all the way. We're going to a summit meeting.

While en route, you can reflect that Mount Rainier was a blazing volcano several hundred thousand years ago, and reached perhaps 2000 feet higher than it does now. Where the peak is now, imagine a coneful of flame. And then imagine a tremendous eruption, with debris and volcanic ash blackening all the blue sky you see. Because Mount Rainier literally blew its top—blasted away 2000 feet of its summit and untold thousands of tons of rock—before it settled down to become the serene mountain you see today.

The Cessna's service ceiling is 14,900, Archer's is 13,650. But this trip is special, so head right on up at your best possible rate of climb. As you gain altitude, you'll be hard-pressed to hold your rate of climb above 1000 feet per minute, and then above 500 fpm, even with the yoke in your lap. But it gets still harder. Anyway, try to climb to and maintain 15,000, and you'll be above Mount Rainier, highest point in the state of Washington. (Don't be surprised if you can't get the altitude, though it can be done. Also, you may learn how easy it is to stall even with the airspeed looking real fat.)

When your DME reads a few tenths over 41 nautical miles from the Olympia OMNI station, there's a strip of green just below the snow level of the mountain (though it isn't visible from a Cessna). Flowers bloom here, and there are thick forests where deer, elk, bears, and other animals find sanctuary. Use radar to check on your relationship to the mountain.

There's a surprise waiting for you at or near the summit of Mount Rainier. I won't tell you what it is. But I guided you all the way here to show it to you. In the Cessna, the surprise requires some flying around the mountain, using all kinds of views, before you can appreciate it. Then, if you dare, fly right smack into all that fleecy snow.

In the Archer the surprise will happen automatically. It's fantastic.

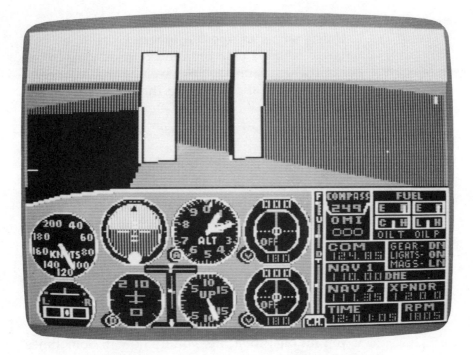

We Aim to
Please

North Position: 17069
East Position: 20984
Altitude: 1200
Pitch: 0
Bank: 0
Heading: 212
Airspeed: 122
Throttle: 19455

Rudder: 32767
Ailerons: 32767
Flaps: 0
Elevators: 32767 (IBM only)
Elevators: 36863 (all except IBM)
Time: 12:00
Season: 2—Spring
Wind: 0 Kts, 0

Hands off controls!
Unless some unexpected breeze kicks in, or you're carrying a case of liquid refreshments in the cockpit which fouls up your weight and balance, the parameters above will do the job. And you'll see New York's World Trade Center towers like no one else has ever seen them before or since.

Take this ride a few times, looking out both sides.

And don't forget the out-the-rear view after the pass. Also look at the angle close-up on radar.
So now you know it can be done.

So now do it yourself. Just crank in a little right or left aileron at the outset, and it's a whole new ball game.
The towers are not figments of the imagination. If you hit one, trust me, you'll know it. Sometimes they seem awesomely close, and you still make it. And sometimes....
Radar doesn't give you an accurate picture of near misses because the radar depiction of your aircraft is not to scale, except in an extreme close-up (such as when you're taking a realistic view of a runway). So, even though it looks like a wing will contact one of those massive walls, you'll still be home free. But too close you *can* come. Your out-the-windshield view is your best guide.
If you absolutely cannot stand crashing, consider that P can stand for *Panic* as well as Pause.
Too, there's always a steep bank available, which just might save that beautiful airplane. And, beautiful or not, the only neck you have.

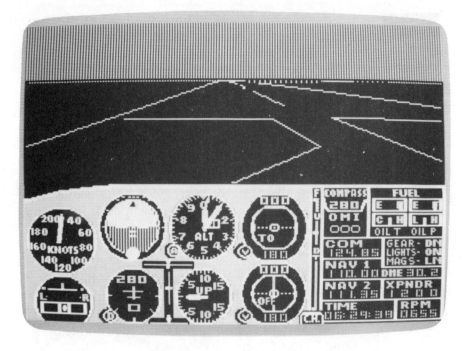

Long Island
It Is

North Position: 17352
East Position: 21751
Altitude: 105
Pitch: 0
Bank: 0
Heading: 280
Airspeed: 0
Throttle: 0

Rudder: 32767
Ailerons: 32767
Flaps: 0
Elevators: 32767
Time: 6:28
Season: 4—Fall
Wind: 3 Kts, 320

It's dawn, and you're right at the base of the 2 of the numbers for runway 28, at Rhode Island's Block Island State Airport.

Daylight turns on in a minute or so—at 6:30. Watch it happen through your windshield. The black landscape suddenly turns green as it's bathed in early sunlight. Beautiful morning to go flying.

And, if you're a bird lover, keep your eyes open. Nearly every northeastern species can be seen here this time of year, since birds use the island as a primary migration checkpoint. It also has fine beaches and is a mecca for bicyclists, fishers, and beachcombers.

We're flying contact this morning, so whenever you're ready take her off. (Watch for the opposite runway numbers to sail by under you.)

Your aircraft is pointed toward the mouth of Long Island Sound.

Stay on your heading of 280 and get straight and level at 2000 feet.

Long Island, New York, is left on your windshield, and the southern edge of Connecticut can be seen on the right. Directly behind you is Block Island. In the far background is Martha's Vineyard, then lots of Atlantic Ocean.

As you fly, add about five to ten degrees to your heading so that the farthest expanse of water lies straight ahead of you, and the landfalls are about equally divided to left and right.

Zoom out to a high altitude radar view to confirm that you're headed straight up the arrowhead of Long Island Sound. Then just keep on keepin' on.

You can pretend it's on automatic pilot if you like and go make yourself a cup of coffee. Or sit back and clip your fingernails. Long Island Sound is a long hunk of water. And Long Island is a heavy piece of geography, as people who ride the Long Island Railroad or drive the Long Island Expressway to Manhattan every day will testify.

And really, that's part of what flying is about, isn't it? The drone of the engine. The only slightly, slowly changing landscape ahead. A point far away on the horizon. A place where sky and water divide exactly in half. It's the kind of thing that gradually bleeds the stresses out of you, like sitting at the end of a fishing pole for a couple of hours or looking at stars.

You can break the monotony by occasionally trying to raise the control tower at Igor I. Sikorski Memorial, 120.9. Maybe this early in the morning Igor Ivanovich (who among other things built the first helicopter in 1939) himself will be operating the microphone. Except he went to the great heliport in the sky in 1972. When you get close enough, anyway, the tower will respond.

 Meanwhile, tune your NAV to Bridgeport VOR, 108.8, and at least you'll know how many miles it is to his airport.

Not that we're going there. But we'll see it.

This is a good trip for practicing things like holding religiously to an altitude, changing altitude, tuning OMNI stations to establish your exact location (your New York/Boston chart is literally buzzing with them), and exploring radar views. Or you might want to practice wagging your wings, power on and power off stalls, climbs and glides, even loops. Whatever it is, you've time on your hands. Just keep getting back to your heading. Visually. Up the Sound. And your altitude, 2000.

Eventually you'll make out a highway zipping in from the right side of your windshield. It's Interstate 91, which joins up with and becomes Interstate 95 where it parallels the shoreline up

39

ahead. It's the same I-95 that eventually bends west and crosses the Hudson River at the George Washington Bridge.

About here you should be able to raise Sikorski, or they'll raise you. To call a station you're tuned to when you think you're in its range, just hit C on the PC, Shift-C on PCjr, and Control-C three times on all other machines.

Keep flying straight toward what seems to be a point where Long Island and Connecticut almost touch. The Sound points to it like an arrowhead.

But it's an optical illusion—or a simulator illusion. As soon as the simulator accesses the disk, you'll see the point disappear. And a radar view will show you're headed more for the shore of Connecticut than you are following the contours of Long Island Sound.

So make a shallow left turn to a heading of about 260, and again you're over open water. Correct again so that you have equal shoreline to left and right and are pointed toward the farthest expanse of open water you can see.

Take a look out your right side now, and perhaps you'll spot Tweed–New Haven Airport, with its runway right at the water's edge.

Then you'll see Sikorski, also with an overwater approach. Your DME will tell you how far out over Long Island Sound you are.

As you pass Sikorsky, take the highest altitude radar view you can (the one before the greenout) and be sure your nose is pointed right up the new arrowhead toward its tip. Make any small corrections necessary to point it there.

The horizon will take on different aspects as you fly the ever-narrowing Sound now. Little juts of land will appear and disappear. And a highway will take shape on the left side of your windshield. That's Interstate 295, which connects Long Island and the Bronx via the Throgs Neck Bridge. Shortly, you'll see the two highways, like snakes, strike at each other across the water. They become one, forming a bridge.

 Check radar now and zoom in a notch closer. You'll see that the bridge is actually two bridges— the nearer one Throgs Neck and the farther one Bronx-Whitestone. The highway across the latter is Interstate 678. Continue to point toward the tip of the arrowhead (right now, beyond the bridges, it becomes a slot).

 A little farther on, try to spot Westchester County Airport out your right side window.

Things will start shaping up now. Keep a lookout for an airport ahead, just a hair to the left of your course. It's La Guardia, named for a wonderfully pixieish mayor (1934–1945) of New York City, Fiorello H. La Guardia, who used to read the Sunday comics to kids over the radio. The airport is just beyond the Throgs Neck and Bronx-Whitestone bridges (those long highwaylike bridges you'll shortly fly over—toll bridges to the ordinary mortals below).

Stay on your heading and let La Guardia slip by slightly to your left. As it does, there's a disk access and you're aimed at the heart of Manhattan.

 Take a look on radar and adjust zoom until you see that the water you're flying over takes a 45-degree turn to the left not far ahead. At that point, it becomes the East River.

 Turn with and track the river. If you've flown certain earlier modes in this book with us, you know that the buildings on your right are, in order, the Empire State Building and the twin towers of the

World Trade Center. The first bridge you see is
the Queensboro Bridge. Directly under that bridge,
but not visible in the simulation, is the southern
end of Roosevelt Island, a small strip of land that
has become a New York City community on its
own. And just beyond Roosevelt Island, though
not visible even if you were standing on the riverbank, the Queens-Midtown Tunnel lopes under
the river.

Two more bridges lie ahead. The nearest one is
the Williamsburg Bridge, and just beyond that, the
river bends to the right and passes under the
Manhattan Bridge. You might want to lose a bit of
altitude to get a closer look.

When you pass Manhattan Bridge—a 3-D feature of the simulation—you're over Upper Bay, at
the mouth of the Hudson River, with the tip of
Manhattan to your immediate right and the Statue
of Liberty probably visible as a dot in the bay.
Worthy of mention is that you've also flown over,
a moment after passing Manhattan Bridge, the
famous Brooklyn Bridge, unseen in the simulation,
but enshrined forever in the poetic inspiration of
Thomas Wolfe who walked it often. (If you are in-
terested, I can make you a deal on the bridge.)

As you approach the middle of the bay, make a
left turn to a heading of 175 degrees. If you lost
altitude earlier, get back to 2000 now.

The land to your left is Brooklyn, and to your
right Staten Island. Beyond these are Lower Bay
and the Atlantic Ocean.

When you're over Lower Bay, turn left again
and head due east. You'll be flying along the
southern shoreline of Long Island.

The airport ahead to your left is John F. Kennedy International. As you fly past it, tune your
NAV to Deer Park OMNI, 111.2, and set your OBI
to fly directly to the station.

Your destination is Republic Airport, about six miles this side of the OMNI.

Since there's no tower in the simulation for Republic, call JFK on 119.1 and check the winds. If there are still none or if they're light, land on the runway of your choice. Runways are 1–19 and 14–32.

Alternative: If you just haven't had enough flying for one morning, continue right up Long Island's southern coastline. It'll point you back to Block Island, and you'll be there in plenty of time for lunch.

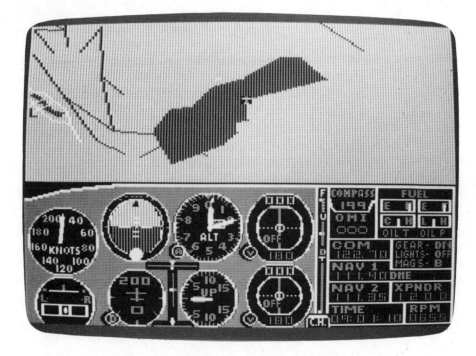

A Place of
Your Own

North Position: 21827
East Position: 6410
Altitude: 82
Pitch: 0
Bank: 0
Heading: 200
Airspeed: 0
Throttle: 0

Rudder: 32767
Ailerons: 32767
Flaps: 0
Elevators: 32767
Time: 9:00
Season: 3—Summer
Wind: 6 Kts, 200

If you're sitting in a Cessna do *not* take any left side views. You're so close to the water you will *splash* into it, since for some strange reason the Microsoft simulator seems to check where you are looking, rather than where you are, in deciding whether or not to give you a drenching. (To prevent the splash, you could set east position to 6409, but that would defeat our purpose.) In the Archer, you can look all around.

This dynamic, geometric abstraction of grass, sea, and sky is no ordinary simulator scenic. You're in a very special place. A place painstakingly carved for you from an otherwise featureless and monotonous landscape.

It's a grass strip, like the old days when pilots were wild-eyed daredevils, and any reasonably long stretch of grass or sandy beach would serve. Only the flying fools and a few kids who came out to watch them knew where it was. And how to get back to it.

But this *flying field* (that's really what it should be called) is no ordinary strip of grass; it's not even in the United States.

You are on your own private runway surrounded by a body of water called Juan de Fuca Strait. Precisely, you are at the southernmost tip of Vancouver Island, British Columbia, Canada. Juan de Fuca Strait is an inlet of the Pacific Ocean which flows for a hundred miles between Vancouver Island and the northwestern corner of the state of Washington. The Canadian–U.S. border is in the middle of the strait.

It's easy to *see* the runway here, for which you're already exactly lined up, if you just imagine a right side which is a mirror image of the left. The water marks the left edge of the strip, and a similar, though imaginary, line on the right side of your windshield marks the right.

Take a view directly to the rear (but not left rear, unless you want to see for yourself what I'm talking about). Note that you're indeed right on the edge of the water. Out the right side, of course, it's all green.

And before you start flying, take a look at yourself on radar. Zoom out until you see the distinct bend of the geography ahead. That's the length of the strip in relation to the strait, and you'll find it's plenty long enough. Zoom out three additional notches, and you'll see the shape of the Juan de Fuca. That's the United States across the way. One more notch (though it shows land which doesn't exist) gives you an idea of your relationship to the nearest U.S. airport, William R. Fairchild International at Port Angeles.

You'll find you can tune three OMNI stations from here, even on the ground—Tatoosh, Bay View, and Paine. So you're not in any wilderness.

Now why not fly the pattern a few times? Since it's your own strip, you can have any pattern you like. I fly a lefthand pattern with a pattern altitude of 1750. Do some takeoffs and landings on runways 2 and 20 and get the feel of the area. Don't forget to use radar to help yourself line up. It's a very distinct spot on the geography.

As a suggestion, make your first takeoff a long one so that you'll have an idea of how far away the water is. Use no flaps. Before you add power for your takeoff run, give two quick strokes of up elevator. Then to start your run, use full power followed immediately by a four-notch power reduction (F2 followed by two F8s if you're flying the PC). Then use no controls until you're airborne.

When the land slips away under your nose, take a look back.

At some point, try a takeoff as above, but use only one quick stroke of up elevator (the Cessna elevator position indicator won't move), followed by full power and then eight notches of power reduction (F2, then four F8s on PC). And wait. The suspense is awful, but you'll see how realistic your private flying field is.

(Believe it or not, in the Cessna one stroke of elevator and power backed off six notches from full will use up all the grass, but will get you safely into the air—by a hair. Try it for thrills.)

You can ink in your Canadian runway on your chart and think of it as a real place. You can give it whatever name you like. And you can fly to and from it from and to anywhere in the Seattle area.

One final thought: Sometime, get into edit mode and change just the hour to something around midnight. You'll see that your private field's runway is marked as clearly as it is in the daytime.

A return trip at night, too, is entirely possible.

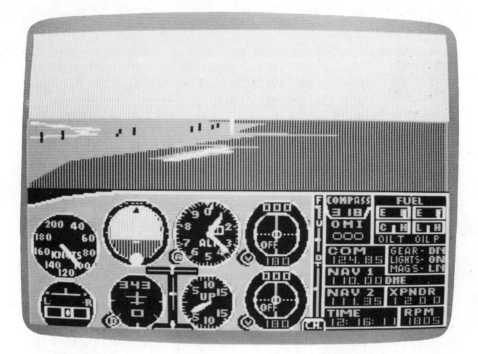

One Good Turn

North Position: 17184
East Position: 16690
Altitude: 1600
Pitch: 0
Bank: 0
Heading: 180
Airspeed: 120
Throttle: 19400

Rudder: 32767
Ailerons: 32767
Flaps: 0
Elevators: 32767 (IBM only)
Elevators: 36863 (all except IBM)
Time: 12:15
Season: 4—Fall
Wind: 5 Kts, 350

Please read the entire text before beginning this flight.

You're in a Meigs righthand pattern downwind for runway 36. You're over Lake Michigan at pattern altitude, which is 1000 AGL nominal (you're at 1008 AGL). A right turn, to a heading of 270, will put you on base. A second right turn, to a heading due north, will put you on final. Great chance here to fly the *box*, and keep flying it until you get the hang of it.

It's no secret nor any surprise that the simulator is harder to land than a real airplane—in some ways. You don't have the natural depth perception, visual clues and perspectives, and other real-world references that you have in an actual aircraft. Our microcomputers are simply not fast or sensitive enough to get our most subtle messages. What, in a real aircraft, is a *little bit* of pressure—with perhaps the thumb—to correct just a *tiny bit* seems to cause the simulator to overreact.

However, we're flying a simulator, not a multi-thousand-dollar real machine (nor a multi-million-dollar simulator), and practice is the only way we'll conquer it.

This mode will save you lots of time getting up there and into position, so you can concentrate on judging and timing your first turn, then judging and timing your second. Both good turns, let's hope, and blended smoothly with flap settings and pitch and power adjustments that put you down right on the numbers.

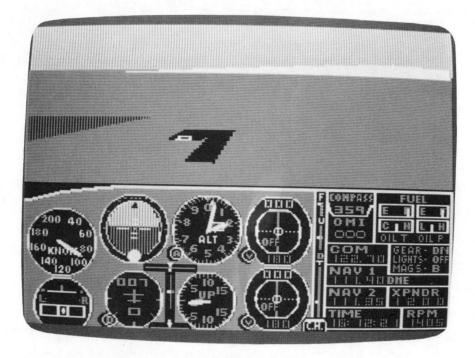

The Mystery
of Sammamish

North Position: 21349
East Position: 6655
Altitude: 1840
Pitch: 359
Bank: 17
Heading: 327
Airspeed: 120
Throttle: 19600

Rudder: 32767
Ailerons: 32767
Flaps: 0
Elevators: 35292 (IBM only)
Elevators: 37887 (all except IBM)
Time: 16:11
Season: 2—Spring
Wind: 5 Kts, 350

51

Hold the bank until you see what looks like an airstrip, then take over at once and land the airplane.

This unusual-looking airport becomes more unusual as you get closer.

Presently, you'll see that the runway—if it is a runway—is a blacktop with no centerline. The whole area between the white lines fills in.

This landing will call for some skill, because your approach is not traditional. It's more of a *barnstorming* approach. At least it'll seem that way, since you've had no chance to get your bearings.

The heading of the strip is 10 degrees and the elevation 496 (maybe that will help).

Once you set her down, use radar and take a look around you. Where are you?

And is this an airport? Taxi around a bit and look it over. If it's an airport, where's the centerline? Even the grass strips in the simulator have centerlines. And what's that big rectangle? It's certainly not a building because it's as flat as the rest of the landscape. And if it's a fuel pump, where's the *F?*

The "Interesting Topographical Features" sheet that comes with *Flight Simulator II* lists Lake Sammamish as one of the interesting topographical features. The Microsoft manual doesn't mention Sammamish or interesting topographical features. And it says nothing about a new airport.

Maybe it's an airport under construction? Or maybe it's an experiment of some kind. Could we have strayed into a top-secret military base?

One thing is certain: It's not a town, because it's too narrow. It's not a road, because it doesn't go anywhere. And it's not a grass strip, because it's too black and hard.

It looks exactly like a runway, with a fuel pump (simulator style), but without a centerline. And with absolutely no fanfare.

And I have some other news for you. The current FAA Seattle Sectional Aeronautical Chart doesn't show an airstrip here either.

So what is this interesting topographical feature on the tip of Lake Sammamish?

I leave you to figure it out.

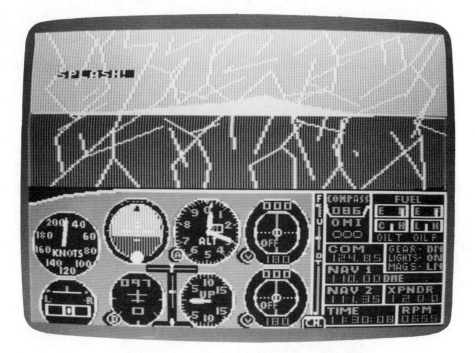

Another Fine Mess

North Position: 21295
East Position: 6477
Altitude: 292
Pitch: 0
Bank: 0
Heading: 98
Airspeed: 0
Throttle: 0

Rudder: 32767
Ailerons: 32767
Flaps: 0
Elevators: 32767
Time: 11:30
Season: 1—Winter
Wind: 5 Kts, 330

Very nice view of Mount Rainier across the water, isn't it? However, you paid dearly to attain this grandstand seat.

Wherever in the world do you think you are?

Perhaps if you get that annoying *splash*, you're exhaling when you should be inhaling. Or perhaps you didn't check your weight and balance properly?

How can you be motionless on the ground and keep falling into the water?

 There *is* a way out, at least the *splash* part of it: Just get into radar mode.

Now, once things seem to have settled down, you can use zoom and see what kind of predicament you got yourself into.

Yes, this is a real runway. It's Tacoma Narrows in the Seattle area. Narrows is a good name for this place. Only an Olympic diving champ could feel at home out here.

 So, anyway, now try an out-the-windshield view again.

Back to the drawing board? Or does the airplane know it's on the runway and not on the water?

Apparently, the simulator looks a bit ahead of your aircraft to decide whether you're going to ditch or not. Because you're surely *on* this runway. And when you're in radar, the simulator must look down from on high, too, rather than out the windshield. Or something like that.

Anyway, you're cleared for departure whenever you're ready.

Honestly, you *can* turn around and take off on runway 35. So do it. But maybe you shouldn't look out the windshield until you have plenty of blacktop under your nosewheel.

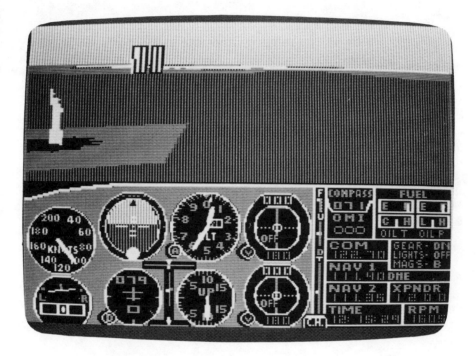

Two on an Island

North Position: 17299	**Rudder:** 32767
East Position: 20983	**Ailerons:** 32767
Altitude: 1300	**Flaps:** 0
Pitch: 0	**Elevators:** 36863 (except IBM)
Bank: 0	**Elevators:** 32767 (IBM only)
Heading: 181	**Time:** 8:15
Airspeed: 121	**Season:** 3—Summer
Throttle: 19455	**Wind:** 0 Kts, 0

This majestic expanse of water is the Hudson River. You're just where the simulator picks it up, Peekskill, New York. About 5 miles behind you is the U.S. Military Academy at West Point, which is on the river. You are about 38 miles north of John F. Kennedy International Airport.

 Follow the river. It has just widened at this point, after flowing a few hundred miles from its source farther north in the Adirondack Mountains.

 For the best vistas, use radar and your out-the-windshield view to fly about midriver.

 Tune your NAV to JFK OMNI, 115.9, which will provide you with a check on distances. About 37 miles out, you should be able to spot Westchester County Airport ahead to your left. It's 7 or 8 miles east of the river.

High altitude radar at about 32 to 33 nautical miles from JFK will show you Long Island Sound at the upper left of your screen, though it's about 25 miles away. The highway along the Sound is I-95.

Twenty miles from JFK you'll spot our old friend La Guardia on the east side of the river, and after another mile or so you'll see Manhattan beginning to take shape.

The first of three tall buildings you see is the Empire State Building, and the other two are the World Trade Center towers—all of which we've seen from other angles in earlier modes. And the gradually enlarging white dot in the river proper is, of course, the Statue of Liberty.

When your DME shows about 16.5 miles, zoom in with a radar view until the black shape of New York City appears. That patch of green in the center is Central Park—a green relief for city dwellers, with jogging and cycling paths, horse-drawn carriages for hire, and the famous Central Park Zoo.

About 14 or 15 miles from Kennedy, views out the left side will give you an excellent picture of downtown New York and the three featured buildings passing by.

Keep your nose pointed straight at the Statue of Liberty. And why not start an approach right now: You're going to land this airplane on Ellis Island, right at the foot of the statue. (And while you're making your approach, see if you notice anything unusual about the Lady Liberty.)

So pull your carb heat on, get into slow flight, and put on a notch of flaps. Point at Liberty just as if it were a runway. Presently the disk will be accessed, and you'll see where you're going. Elevation of Ellis Island is 430 feet.

Make a full-flaps landing just to the right of the statue, as close to the near side of the island as you can manage. You probably won't use up even half the grass.

You can't see the statue too well from inside the cockpit and up this close. So taxi to some edge of the island, as close to the water as is safe, turn around, apply your brakes, and you'll see at least a reasonable portion of the base. (Too bad you can't get out the door!)

When you've enjoyed the view (and checked carb heat off, elevator centered), taxi the aircraft to what you feel is your best position for a short field takeoff, then execute the takeoff using your best information. (Note that there is no wind.) Keep your brakes on until you have maximum rpm. When you're safely airborne, be sure to look back at the statue. Beautiful.

See you at Kennedy.

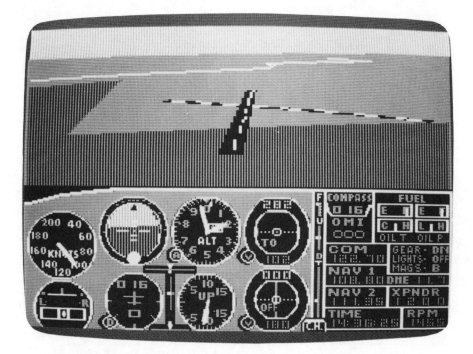

Water Ballet

North Position: 17250
East Position: 21327
Altitude: 2500
Pitch: 0
Bank: 0
Heading: 21
Airspeed: 122
Throttle: 19450

Rudder: 32767
Ailerons: 32767
Flaps: 0
Elevators: 36863 (except IBM)
Elevators: 32767 (IBM only)
Time: 14:30
Season: 3—Summer
Wind: 6 Kts, 0

You're over Long Island Sound, inbound for runway 2 at Tweed–New Haven.

But the tower advises you must stop short of the intersection, since workers are repairing a pothole exactly where the runways cross. "Clear to land if you can comply."

"Roger, no problem," you say, with a nonchalance that indicates you've been jockeying airplanes around the sky for at least 20 years. But the way your knuckles go white on the yoke isn't too comforting.

You'll see the strip ahead in a few minutes. You're going to wish it was absolutely straight ahead. But of course it isn't. The reason you wish it were straight ahead is because this is one of those runways that extend over the water. No landing on the grass here. The resultant *splash* would be worse than the *clumph* of a nosewheel in a pothole.

So you're committed to getting lined up *very* precisely. You'd hate to have to go around, having convinced the tower that you started flying back when Eddie Rickenbacker threw a pigeon from his cockpit into an overcast to see if it got disoriented. (It did, so the story goes, and started flying reasonably only when it fell below the clouds and had visual reference to the ground.)

Simulator runways do seem to dance around a lot, don't they? That "2.5-inch resolution" (of what?) the manual talks about often seems more like 2.5 miles. You think you're a little to the right, so you correct a little to the left, then you think you're a little to the left, so you....

Anyway, you can return to this mode anytime you feel like practicing to improve your precision. Or to see if maybe your precision improved by itself while you weren't paying any attention to it.

Decisions,
Decisions

North Position: 21305
East Position: 6508
Altitude: 10000
Pitch: 359
Bank: 0
Heading: 14
Airspeed: 122
Throttle: 0

Rudder: 32767
Ailerons: 32767
Flaps: 0
Elevators: 36863 (except IBM)
Elevators: 32767 (IBM only)
Time: 12:35
Season: 4—Fall
Wind: 15 Kts, 30

Here you are, ten thousand feet over Seattle and your engine dies. (You may *not* use throttle!)

Glad at least you have some altitude, hmmm? Chance to think. Time to use all your resources—radar, chart, out-the-windshield views, your flying skills, and judgment.

Set her down safely at the airport of your choice. A landing on the grass somewhere or crossways on a runway or even on a city street is better than no landing at all—or than a ditching. Still, you're only a winner if you manage the runway you decide on at the outset.

Good luck.

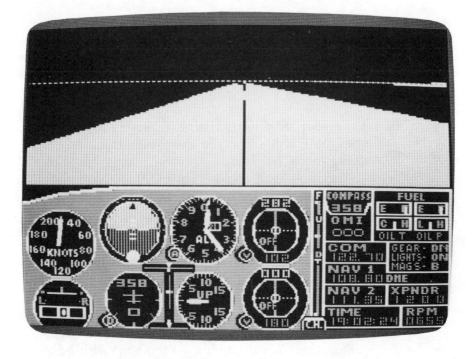

Night Has a Thousand Eyes

North Position: 21371
East Position: 6481
Altitude: 370
Pitch: 0
Bank: 0
Heading: 40
Airspeed: 0
Throttle: 0

Rudder: 32767
Ailerons: 32767
Flaps: 0
Elevators: 32767
Time: 19:00
Season: 1—Winter
Wind: 4 Kts, 330

The area is Seattle, and the airport is Port Orchard Airport, Washington, on the west side of Puget Sound. You're in position to taxi onto runway 36 for a night flight to Snohomish County Airport (Paine Field).

Tune your NAV to the Paine VOR, 114.2, and your DME will show you the distance you'll be flying.

Also, go ahead and set your OBI to fly directly to the station. What heading will you take up when you've departed Port Orchard?

Before you leave, get into radar and zoom out. The large body of water on three sides (though it looks like land) is the Sound, and the highways on the other side are Interstates 5 and 405. Interstate 5 goes to Seattle and continues north. Interstate 405 goes to Bellevue, which is across Lake Washington from Seattle, and then joins up with I-5.

Your flight will take you across Puget Sound and over the northern outskirts of Seattle. The airport is a few miles ahead and to the left of where the highways join.

Take off when you're ready. Since your cruising altitude will be above 3000 feet, observe the regulations:

Heading 0–179 degrees: altitude = odd thousands + 500
Heading 180–359 degrees: altitude = even thousands + 500

So, cruise at 3500.

After the disk access, you can see how I-5 and I-405 merge ahead of you. They point the way (though it's rather difficult to separate them visually from the coastline in the simulation).

Hold your altitude and keep the needle centered.

When your DME reads about 20, tune Snohomish ATIS, 128.65, and see what's what.

If the winds haven't shifted, they're probably landing on runway 29, so begin thinking about your approach. Assume a lefthand traffic pattern. If you're not familiar with it, the traffic pattern around a small airport can be visualized as a series of 90-degree turns, creating a box. The active runway represents, of course, the heading for both takeoff and final approach, also called the *upwind leg*. After takeoff, the first 90-degree turn, whether left or right, puts you on the *crosswind leg*. The next 90-degree turn puts you on the *downwind leg*, and the next on the *base leg*. The last turn puts you on *final* (final approach).

In the simulator, since we have no actual conversations with the tower (except for standard advisories and active runway information where available), I regard all airports as "small" airports and fly the small-airport traffic pattern. With similar bravado, I decide whether they are flying a right- or lefthand pattern to suit myself. Then (sometimes, but certainly not always) I enter the pattern at a 45-degree angle with the imagined traffic. Or, depending on my heading, I simply squeeze myself onto whatever leg is convenient.

There's a product available at most small airports called PDQ (there are other equivalent products, I'm sure). It's a Visual Airport Guide consisting of three plastic pieces riveted together like a circular slide rule. PDQ allows you to visualize your aircraft heading, the runway heading, 45-degree entry angles, and the traffic pattern you're going to enter. What it does, essentially, is eliminate the math involved in deciding what headings put you on what legs, thus, simplifying your entry into a pattern. It answers very quickly questions like "what's base for runway 29?"

Just happen to have that information right here.

67

Base for a runway heading of 290 and a lefthand pattern is 20 degrees. So, since you're now heading somewhere in the vicinity of 6 degrees, think about a shallow right turn to base when the time comes.

When Snohomish is 17 to 18 miles ahead, it'll become visible on your windshield. Time to start planning your letdown.

A high altitude radar view, even this far out, will show you the airport (the big airports get all the breaks in the simulator; sometimes it seems like the little ones never show up).

The elevation at Snohomish is 603 feet. Pattern altitude (normally 800 to 1000 feet AGL) would thus be about 1400 indicated, minimum. Sounds okay for base leg.

The FAA sectional shows Snohomish is about five miles north of the Interstate 5/405 junction, so plan your turn to base accordingly, using radar and/or right side views of the junction.

You'd be well advised to get into classic approach configuration for this landing for several reasons. It's night. Runway 29 is the least conspicuous of the runways. You're tired.

So, don't have too much speed; do have some flaps on base leg; watch for the depiction of the runway on radar; and, remember, it's going to be at 90 degrees to your heading.

Take out-the-windshield views so that you always know where the airport is; take ever-closer-in radar views until you know which runway you're bound for; don't get dazzled by the lights; note that Martha Lake strip is across the highway from the threshold of 29; don't forget the carb heat; try to have at least 1000 feet indicated when you turn final; and don't wait too long to do that; and let's see, what else? Oh, yes—don't forget your umbrella. It might be raining in Snohomish.

And once you're on the ground, have a look at all those lights—out the windshield and on radar.

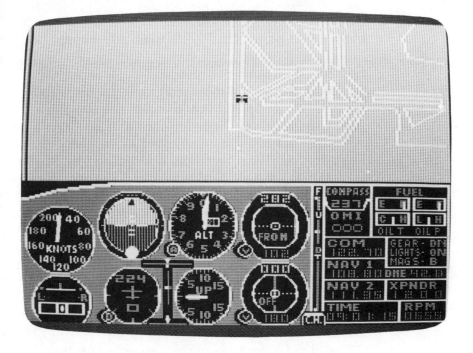

The Great Beyond

North Position: 17029
East Position: 21073
Altitude: 13
Pitch: 0
Bank: 0
Heading: 224
Airspeed: 0
Throttle: 0

Rudder: 32767
Ailerons: 32767
Flaps: 0
Elevators: 32767
Time: 9:00
Season: 2—Spring
Wind: 6 Kts, 180

Ever wonder what lies beyond the charts? What happens if you fly 20, 30, 40 miles off the page?

So have I. So this nice spring morning let's both find out. With your permission, I'll ride with you. I'll record the whole trip exactly as it happens (in realtime, no less!), right on this and the ensuing pages, so we'll both have a record of it.

We may be going nowhere, but at least let's leave in style. We're positioned for takeoff on runway 22, left, at New York's John F. Kennedy International Airport. (Precisely, we're heading 224 to 225 degrees. I know we're a bit off-center, but this is a wide runway.)

Tune your NAV to the Kennedy VORTAC, 115.9, and set the flag to FROM, if it's not already reading that, so we'll have a distance reference. You don't have to center the needle, because we're going to fly contact.

The idea I have is to make a straight-out departure from Kennedy. Our takeoff will be over Jamaica Bay, and if we hold the 224-degree heading, we'll fly straight toward New Jersey's Sandy Hook, which you can see in the lower-left corner of the New York–Boston area chart. A turn directly to the south as we approach Sandy Hook will point us straight down the New Jersey coast, with the seashore resorts on our right and the Atlantic Ocean on our left.

Let's give it a whirl. Go ahead and take off.

We can see the water as soon as we have a hundred feet or so of altitude. And before the DME reads one nautical mile, we can see—land, ho!

Let's level off at 3000. That seems like an optimum altitude for our observations.

Radar views, from either high or low altitude, can be deceptive. For instance, if we take a high altitude view over Lower Bay, which we reach a few minutes after takeoff, the Atlantic Ocean has turned to green grass. Either that or there's an awful lot of seaweed out there. But in its own time the simulator develops what it wants to develop for us. As I scribe this, I have no idea whether it'll be grass from here on or not. Remember, while I'm writing this I'm experiencing it for the first time just like you.

Well, there was just a disk access, wasn't there? The DME reads 7-odd nautical miles from Kennedy. Is that goodbye to everything? Or hello, New Jersey? The manual *does* say that the simulation covers 10,000 × 10,000 miles. Not in great detail, maybe. But I'll settle if I see a coastline and an Atlantic Ocean for 20 or 30 or 40 miles.

I'm wondering what that little black dot is, left of center on the shoreline ahead.

Now, suddenly (believe me, exactly as I write this), there's what looks like a city or a large airport ahead. I haven't a clue as to what it is. The DME reads between 12 and 13. The heading is still 224. And we're at 3000.

But it's a phantom. As suddenly as it appeared, it's gone. Did you see that? Was it Atlantis? A sea monster? A mother ship swooping in for reconnaissance?

Well, the black dot's gone, too.

At 21.6 from Kennedy, I have the dot in sight again, and I've come to a conclusion. It's simply one of those jagged shoreline points entering the simulation. Each one starts as a dot, I guess. Do you agree?

Take a look on radar. Still nothing of interest.

It occurs to me that we should be over land by now. In fact, we should have been over land about 10 miles ago. New Jersey is only about 17 miles from Kennedy on this heading. Something is amiss.

Turn left to a heading of 180.

Switch in your radar and experiment some.

There's a shoreline, all right, and we're flying alongside it. But toward what? More of that massive seaweed. So thick you could cut it with a lawn mower.

And look out the left side. More of the same. Unless we're looking at Spain there across the Atlantic. It's certainly not Long Island this far south.

Try a view straight back.

Now that makes some sense. That looks like where we've come from. Is it possible that if we flew TO rather than from JFK along the Jersey coast, we'd have more realism?

But for the moment let's continue straight ahead and see if anything opens up. Let's fly south until the DME reads 40.

Better yet, let's fly until we see if the seaweed ahead opens up. If you check radar, you'll see we're headed for a world of green. What'll happen when we cross that line of demarcation and leave the ocean behind us?

Perhaps it's a new overseas highway Bruce Artwick has fashioned.

One thing is sure, if it's earth, we should be able to land on it. Are you game? If you are, check radar until you're sure you're over land, then set her down straight ahead. That's what I'm doing.

A nice flat approach makes sense, because we have no idea of the altitude of this place. And zilch in the way of visual references. Below a thousand feet, try to set up a descent rate of 500 feet per minute or less, with a speed just above stalling. And simply wait, because you'll have no idea when you should flare. At least I don't think so.

Now, 700...600...500...400...300...200—if it gets close to 0 then perhaps it's right AT sea level, so you can flare after all—100...75...50...

Well, now, what do you think of that? That's what I call high-protein seaweed!

Perhaps you want to quit now. Or maybe turn around and fly back up the coast to see if the perspective is different and the world more real going that way. That's what I'm going to do.

 But, first, let's true the altimeter and go into the edit mode to check what altitude we're actually sitting on.

Hmmph! Must be low tide.

My conclusion from this trip is that the part of the simulator world which isn't on the area charts is, ultimately, all green. A few miles or minutes beyond the edges of the charts is a Great Beyond of green. A green North Pole. A green Siberia. A green Indian Ocean.

But I have a suggestion (submitted humbly indeed): The Great Beyond should be blue.

For blue is what this little aimless speck of dust in the infinity is and what it appears to be when seen from elsewhere. Blue. The blue of water. The pale blue of polar ice. The blue of distant mountains. The blue of nearly 140 million square miles of oceans, lakes, and waterways.

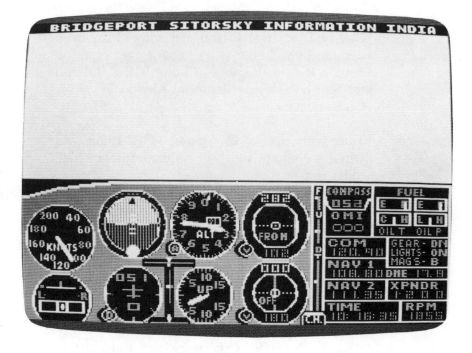

Falling Off a Log

North Position: 17165
East Position: 21167
Altitude: 3000
Pitch: 0
Bank: 0
Heading: 56
Airspeed: 122
Throttle: 19455

Rudder: 32767
Ailerons: 32767
Flaps: 0
Elevators: 32767 (IBM only)
Elevators: 36863 (all except IBM)
Time: 10:15
Season: 4—Fall
Wind: 7 Kts, 300

Add for this mode:
Cloud Layer 1: Tops, 4000; Bottoms, 2400

77

You were VFR when suddenly things got kind of cloudy. Don't worry. You just entered the overcast, and you know you're about over Huntington Bay on the north shore of Long Island, inbound for Igor I. Sikorsky Memorial Airport in Connecticut.

Tune your NAV to Bridgeport VOR, 108.8, and you'll see you're right on course and about 20 miles out.

Contact the Sikorski control tower on 120.9 to see where the bottom of the overcast is and what runway is active.

Your request for a descent to 2000 is approved by the tower, so back off your power and get down there where you can see again.

Once you have the Connecticut shoreline in sight, keep a lookout for the airport. Since the OMNI is right there, Sikorski should show up straight ahead on your course. It's right at the water's edge.

When you're ready, a shallow right turn to a heading of 70 degrees will put you on base for runway 34. Field elevation is a mere ten feet.

A few checks out the side; judicious application of pitch, power, and flaps; a nicely executed left turn—you'll be right on the money.

Now doesn't that sound easy?

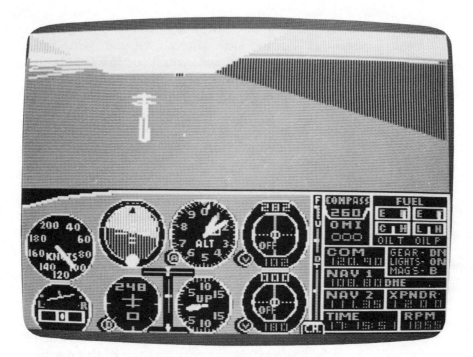

Circle Around
Dinner

North Position: 21414
East Position: 6599
Altitude: 1200
Pitch: 358
Bank: 344
Heading: 348
Airspeed: 109
Throttle: 19455 (IBM only)
Throttle: 17407 (all except IBM)

Rudder: 32767
Ailerons: 32767
Flaps: 0
Elevators: 33279 (IBM only)
Elevators: 37887 (all except IBM)
Time 17:15
Season: 4—Fall
Wind: 3 Kts, 360

As soon as you exit edit mode, take a 90-degree view out your left side. Directly off your wing tip, as the mode settles down, you'll see the Seattle Space Needle. And it'll pretty much stay there without your touching the controls.

Apply a little left aileron to steepen the bank if it unsteepens. You may also need minor power adjustments to hold your altitude.

Your aircraft is performing a shallow, slow-speed, wide-radius turn around a point (flying in a circle while keeping a specific landmark or target in view and in the same relative position). This is a very valuable maneuver to have in your repertoire and is always included early in flight instruction curricula. It doesn't take much imagination to see how valuable this type of turn can be in everyday flying.

You can almost see inside the restaurant, which is in the observation tower at the top of the needle. It's dinner time, and the patrons can't fail to notice your low-altitude shenanigans over the tops of their heads.

After you've made a few circuits, and maybe watched the maneuver on radar, too, take over completely.

Experiment with the concept of the turn. Try a steeper bank and different pitch and power settings, the object being always to keep the needle—the point—right where it is off your left wing tip. See if you can tighten the circle or change the perspective of your view. Practice until you feel comfortable with the maneuver.

Straighten up, fly around, then come back and see if you can set up the turn yourself, but turning to the right this time. If you can, you'll have something to celebrate at your own favorite café after you land.

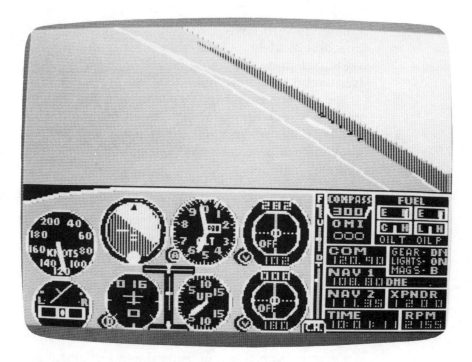

High Jinks

North Position: 17060
East Position: 16584
Altitude: 6000
Pitch: 0
Bank: 0
Heading: 43
Airspeed: 127 (IBM only)
Airspeed: 117 (all except IBM)
Throttle: 25591 (IBM only)

Throttle: 21495 (all except IBM)
Rudder: 32767
Ailerons: 32767
Flaps: 0
Elevators: 32767 (IBM only)
Elevators: 37887 (all except IBM)
Time: 10:00
Season: 3—Summer
Wind: 6 Kts, 000

Pointed toward Lake Michigan, in the general direction of Meigs, this is your practice mode for stalls and stunts. You're straight and level at a (relatively) safe altitude.

You can try anything you want; then simply press the reset simulator key (Recall on the IBM) and try it again. And again. The mode will always get you back up to altitude (and out of any trouble you might get into).

 First, read, then try this stall: Cut your power completely. Then increase up elevator gradually, trying to achieve and maintain a slightly nose-high attitude. This will require more and more elevator. Eventually, your angle of attack will become too great (you'll hear the stall warning a few seconds before this happens), and the nose will drop rather abruptly below the horizon.

You've stalled.

Recover from the stall using down elevator until the elevator indicator is at its normal cruise position, thus reducing your angle of attack. (This is comparable to, in an actual aircraft, eliminating back pressure so that the yoke returns to its normal position.)

After you've normalized the elevator, add full power until you have the usual horizon again. Then reduce power until the throttle indicator is at your normal cruise setting; reestablish straight and level flight. The less altitude lost during the stall, the better you performed the recovery.

The preceding is called a *normal power-off stall.*

 First, read, then try this loop: Give full down elevator until you pin the airspeed indicator at maximum. Smoothly (and not too quickly) add up elevator to the three-quarters-up position. When there is only the sky in view, apply full throttle and take a left or right side view. You'll see your-

self flying toward the top of the loop, about to become inverted. Just before you're completely
upside down (wings level with horizon), take a
front view and see the earth upside down. When
you see only ground, cut throttle completely.
Then, when you see the horizon, add throttle and
adjust elevator to resume normal flight.

Quick summary (Loop from normal cruise):
Full down elevator: Maximum speed
Smoothly: Three-quarters-up elevator
Sky only: Full throttle, side view
Almost inverted: Front view
Downside (earth only): Chop throttle
See horizon: Add throttle, adjust elevator

With some practice, you'll surely catch on. Then
try mixing up the views.
Fun, hmmm?

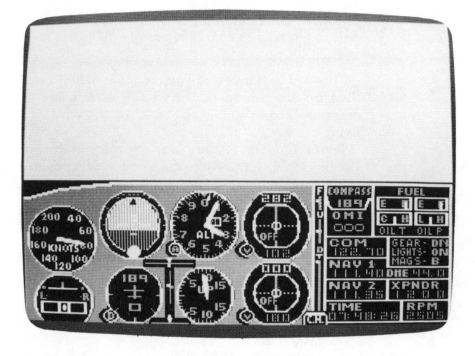

Goldilocks

North Position: 15402
East Position: 5955
Altitude: 296
Pitch: 0
Bank: 0
Heading: 190
Airspeed: 0
Throttle: 0

Rudder: 32767
Ailerons: 32767
Flaps: 0
Elevators: 32767
Time: 7:45
Season: 1—Winter
Wind: 2 kts, 180

Add for this mode:
Cloud Layer 2: Tops, 5000; Bottoms, 2000
Cloud Layer 1: Tops, 1500; Bottoms, 300

Be sure to check heading when you exit edit mode. And do not read this mode before you fly it. You'll spoil all the fun.

This had to happen to you, on a day when even the birds are grounded. The whole Los Angeles area is socked in so bad not even the flags are flying.

But on Catalina Island—way out there in the Pacific Ocean, somewhere out there in this potato soup, a little golden-haired girl is desperately ill. She's been bitten by a rare type of Pacific tick. Without a special serum available only here on the mainland, she may not live another 12 hours.

No pilot in his right mind would dream of flying serum to Catalina in weather like this. So they turned to you.

And how could you refuse a little golden-haired girl the chance of life?

Yes, you'd go.

So here you are at El Monte Airport. (Regard your radar as *disabled* for this flight.)

You know you're lined up okay for takeoff, because you went out and got down on your hands and knees with a special fog flashlight to find the centerline. You're somewhere near it. You know the runway heading is 190, and how to take off, because you've done it on lots of sunny days. You know there's a little thousand-foot slot between the cloud layers, and that from 5000 feet on up the ceiling's unlimited. You also know that from 1500 feet on down to 300 feet the overcast is unlimited.

You know still more. You know that Catalina has Santa Catalina OMNI, and you can tune it on 111.4. In addition, you know that there are two ambulances waiting for you on the island, though you can't imagine why they'd have two. And, finally, you know that the little golden-haired girl has said she'd even give you her dolly if you ever get there with the serum.

So, climb in the airplane. If you can find the door. (This stuff's so thick even the density altitude must have doubled.)

Set your NAV to Santa Catalina OMNI and get a heading. (Almost the runway heading, hmm? Every little bit helps.)

Take off in the normal manner. (The altimeter tells you that you did, else who'd ever know?) If things seem a little bleak, note that nice blue over the red on the artificial horizon.

You'll be looking for that thousand-foot slot be-tween the layers. But will you see it?

When you do see it, it isn't all that inviting after all. The deepest blue you ever saw.

Might as well climb on up to five. Ah, now *that's* a blue! Why not level off at 5500? This part of the ride, at least, will be nifty.

Now, as the miles tick by, you can start think-ing about what you'll do when you get to Cat-alina. One thing is sure: If it's as socked in as El Monte, you'll never find the runway. So what are you doing up here in the first place? Even Spencer Tracy wouldn't get himself in a mess like this.

Should you turn around and go back? But to what? Takeoff is one thing. Landing is a whole other ball game. Why are you here? Where's your common sense? Where's your logic? Do you have even a prayer of getting out of this thing alive?

What to do when you get to Catalina? What a joke. You might as well be going to Tibet.

Well, let's figure how to make the best of a really rotten situation.

We're on the beam for Catalina. At the very worst, we might make a blind landing wherever on the island we happen to come down. Just let down and follow the needle and make a normal landing in the soup, just about at zero DME. We'd almost surely hit—I mean reach—the island if we plan on zero DME. That's the ace-in-the-hole.

 Why not let down now and fly in the black slot? Just above the clouds. We'll be at a lower altitude and can time the letdown easier. Black sky's no worse than blue sky in this monstrosity. Yes, descend to 1900.

Keep that needle centered. Last thing you want to do is get off course. Want to head strrrraight for that island as a bare minimum.

Come to think of it, now, if Catalina's at 1602 feet, and we're at 1900, we're only about 300 feet above Catalina's elevation. Now isn't *that* interesting! That means if this altitude-clouds thing is legit, we ought to be able to *see* Catalina sticking up out of the clouds. The tops of the bottom layer of clouds are *below* the Catalina elevation.

So, if the island's sitting there above the clouds, we go ahead and make a landing.

And if the airport *isn't* sticking up out of the clouds when we're a few miles out, the only thing to do is make our best possible slow landing straight ahead, blind, and on our heading. And hope. At zero DME or as close to that as possible.

And those, dear reader, are the best possible solutions in light of all the circumstances.

Please believe I wouldn't ask you to do anything I wouldn't do. And I assure you I made exactly the flight described herein. What's more, without looking at radar until I was on the ground, I landed safely on Catalina (okay, yeah, the island) the first time I made the flight. And I can prove it. A little golden-haired girl is alive today solely because of my heroism.

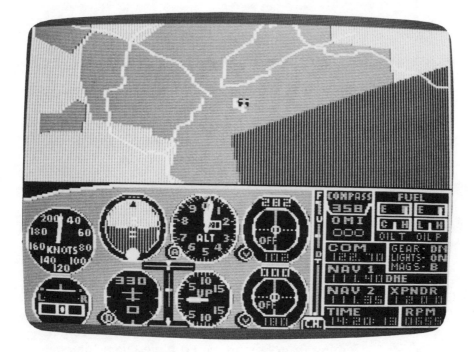

Over on the Mayflower

North Position: 17901
East Position: 21856
Altitude: 23
Pitch: 0
Bank: 0
Heading: 330
Airspeed: 0
Throttle: 0

Rudder: 32767
Ailerons: 32767
Flaps: 0
Elevators: 32767
Time: 14:19
Season: 2—Spring
Wind: 3 Kts, 300

Your takeoff will be from runway 33 at Boston's Logan Airport, named for General Edward Lawrence Logan. (Who, you ask, was General Edward Lawrence Logan? For that piece of triva you'll have to wait till the end of this flight.)

This is the shortest runway at Logan, so you can sit there for a few minutes without worrying about jets whooshing over your head and spraying your plane with kerosene.

 Go into radar and zoom out until you have the upper-left corner of a rectangle of blue behind you and a little green on the left of your screen. The blue is a piece of Boston Harbor, where the water has tasted a bit like tea for a couple of hundred years (some of the tea from the party was actually preserved and is on display in Boston's Old State House).

The airport is a bit northeast of Boston center. Coming from Boston, you'd have taken Interstate 93, which is the highway snaking up on your left, and then a tunnel under a little finger of water which doesn't show on radar. The highway directly ahead of you is U.S. 1, which connects with I-93 at about eleven o'clock from your position. The highway farther west is I-95, which traverses the east coast from Maine to Florida.

 Tune your NAV to Boston VORTAC, 112.7, and set the OBI to read FROM on the runway heading. Your DME, which now reads about 0.6 nautical miles, will serve us as a mutual distance reference.

When you're ready, take off and climb straight out to about 1000 feet. Then, still climbing, do the better part of a 180 to the left, rolling out so that a green patch pointing into Massachusetts Bay is straight ahead of you.

Level off at 3000.

As you fly, go into radar and zoom out until you see a piece of land ahead that looks like the nose of a Concorde on final.

 Before you leave radar, use a little left aileron to point your aircraft toward the tip of the big bird's nose. You'll probably find you're heading somewhere in the general vicinity of 130, but the exact number isn't at all critical.

You'll have nothing but the horizon where sky meets ocean for awhile, but keep flying.

When your DME reads around 14 miles, a bar of green will intermittently spring part way across your windshield from the right, paralleling the horizon. After popping in and out a few times, it'll pop in and stay put. The tip of it will be to the right of your course, but don't change course. Do, however, check radar once in awhile to see that you're still heading for the nose of the Concorde.

 At about 20 miles out, check radar and zoom in another notch. The nose will rear up like something bit the bird.

After several more miles, the end of the bar paralleling the horizon (after a few tentative strikes) will seem to break off and form an island. Then it'll join up with itself again and be two adjacent bars. While this happens, the bars will move closer to the center of your windshield, too. This little episode will repeat itself as you fly. You're simply seeing more and more of the landfall, which is Cape Cod.

At about 34 miles out, zoom in another notch on your radar and again check that you're pointed toward the tip of the peninsula. As your DME creeps toward 37 miles, the tip should be just about in the center of your windshield. Just when it appears there depends on how exactly you're flying up the nose of the big bird.

At 37 miles out, at any rate, back off your throttle a few notches to lose some altitude.

What your aircraft is pointed at is the extreme tip of Cape Cod, and of the state of Massachusetts. The very tip itself has a name: Race Point. Tiny, desolate, and almost surrounded by ocean, Race Point is a wind-whipped, lonely promontory, where, as Thoreau said, "All America is at your back."

Two miles southeast of Race Point is a fishing town with a most interesting history: Provincetown, Massachusetts.

As you continue your descent, give a touch of right aileron so that you're aimed just a little bit to the right of Race Point. This will take you directly over Provincetown.

You won't see it in the simulation, but you're also going to fly over a hill, called Monument Hill because there's a tall monument there. In a moment, we'll find out what it's a monument about.

As the landfall begins to slip under your nose, take a view directly below you, not a radar view, but a ground view, which at this moment shows you not ground, but the water you're flying over.

Now immediately rest your finger on, and be ready to press, P for Pause. Then, when land appears directly below you, press the P.

What you're looking down at is a very historic piece of coastline. For, on the stretch of beach below you, on November 11, 1620, the Pilgrims from the Mayflower made their first landing. And just offshore, in the cabin of the ship (and, one might say, in their first act of chauvinism on this side of the Atlantic), the male passengers of the Mayflower signed the Mayflower Compact, naming themselves and their families a body politic and establishing a local government.

The monument on Monument Hill in Province-town is, of course, a memorial to the Pilgrims.

 Unpause when you're ready, and fly back either to Logan International or, if you feel like it, down to Martha's Vineyard. In either case, Pilgrim or not, demand an excellent landing of thyself.

For you triva fans: Logan International Airport is named for General Edward Lawrence Logan. General Logan held various offices in Boston, but is best known for his work on behalf of the poor and for his military leadership in the Spanish-American War and World War I. His combination of civic work and military activities led to the airport being named for him. He died in 1939.

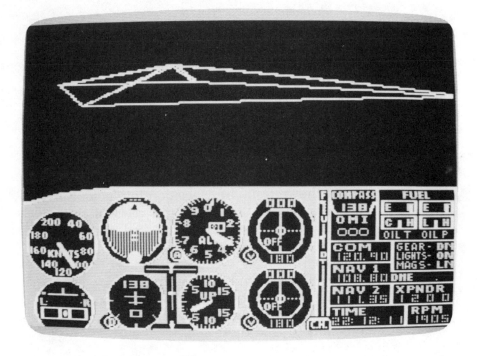

Pyramid Power

North Position: 15303
East Position: 6041
Altitude: 3392
Pitch: 0
Bank: 0
Heading: 139
Airspeed: 118
Throttle: 21503

Rudder: 32767
Ailerons: 32767
Flaps: 0
Elevators: 32767 (IBM only)
Elevators: 36863 (all except IBM)
Time: 22:11
Season: 3—Summer
Wind: 8 Kts, 180

*The phenomenon described below was discovered by
the author using Microsoft's Flight Simulator with
an IBM PC. It seems to have no counterpart in the
SubLogic simulators, unless, of course, you find one.
Otherwise, find a friend with a Cessna so that you
can experience this adventure.* —Editor

Strange apparition in the night sky. Don't touch
the controls. Wait and see what develops from
this transparent geodesic of the gods, this fantasia
of devil's triangles.

See the fantastic transposition into gold. Sure
enough, the devil is behind this celestial alchemy,
this twisted travesty on reality. And what is the
roseate river beyond the shape?

Fly on.

Now like a giant bug awaiting its prey. Now
like a baited web to entrance and entrap. And
again like the closing moments of a raging sunset
on a lonely sand dune.

Perhaps we are extremely far from this entity. Indeed, a look out the right front shows us what may
be a giant space station that a ship has lately left,
with its fiery trail still suspended in the night sky.

Watch the time carefully. We may be in a time
warp.

At 22:16 exactly, go into radar. Zoom out once,
twice, three times. And three times more.

Yes, we are in a black *something.* We're not flying toward it, but are a part of it. We are, in fact,
inside a pyramid. We have somehow entered it,
and we are flying toward the other side. And it is
infinitely more massive than it looks from inside.
As for steepness, consider what your altimeter
tells you.

Yet, when and how and where did we enter this
strange abstraction? We seemed to be outside it
and heading toward it, when suddenly it changed

to its golden outline and turned inward on itself. And took us with it.

Now back to out-the-windshield and, yes, we are aiming for the stream of light beyond the far wall of this translucent lunacy. To what? From what?

Is civilization out there ahead of us? Where the rose line streaks across the sky? And if so, what *kind* of civilization?

When the last vestige, the final fragment, of this structure you have passed through disappears off your windshield, I suggest you go no farther. Instead, at exactly 22:22:22, take a look behind you to confirm what you have done. Then abort. Exit to edit mode. Choose another mode. Shut down for the night. Something. But fly no farther.

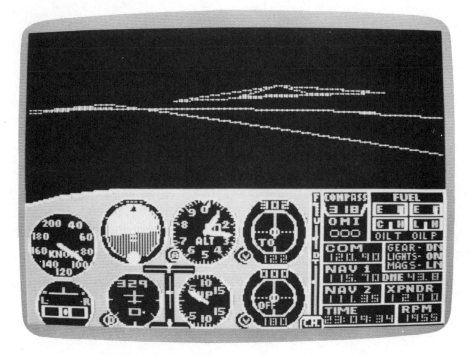

Blues in the
Night

North Position: 14974
East Position: 6098
Altitude: 28
Pitch: 0
Bank: 0
Heading: 243
Airspeed: 0
Throttle: 0

Rudder: 32767
Ailerons: 32767
Flaps: 0
Elevators: 32767
Time: 23:00
Season: 3—Summer
Wind: 4 Kts, 210

There are these blue runways in the IBM version of the simulator. I prefer to think they're moonlit. I like them because they're easier to spot from the air and somehow seem more realistic. Perhaps they are a later development of the constantly changing simulation. Maybe someday we'll even see a paved JFK Airport in New York. (JFK is, after all, not exactly one of your hometown grass strips.)

Whether in an Archer or Cessna, you're in good position to get lined up for runway 24, here at Oceanside Municipal in California, though in the SubLogic version only one side of the runway has its lights working. Your takeoff will be over the ocean or, to be exact, the Gulf of Santa Catalina. You're all gassed up for a night flight to another blue-runway airport, El Monte, northeast of Los Angeles. You've met El Monte before in this book, but not at night.

 Before you taxi out (Archer pilots are already there; check the position on the radar), tune your NAV to Seal Beach VOR, 115.7. You may be too far out of range to get a heading, but the DME will give you a distance readout.

You can tell, using your chart and a straight-edge, that a course of 300 degrees will take you toward Seal Beach, so you'll fly that heading until you pick up the station.

Plan to turn right to your heading as you pass through 1500. Your cruise altitude will be 4500. Ready when you are.

Taxi into position and take off. After you get your exact heading, you're right over the coastline all the way to the Seal Beach OMNI. The road bending in from your left toward all those lights is Interstate 15. The highway more or less paralleling the coast is Interstate 5.

The first city on your route is Santa Ana, where there's an airport curiously named after John Wayne, otherwise, Orange County Airport.

You may want to tune in the Duke's tower for a weather check on 126.0.

Adjust your OBI as you fly, and you'll see (if you're heading 300) that it agrees with your course.

The next big metropolitan area is, of course, Los Angeles. But the airport you see almost straight ahead, at about 25 miles from the Seal Beach VOR, isn't Los Angeles International. It's Meadowlark. Watch for its beacon. Your heading should take you directly over the runway.

El Monte Airport is north of Seal Beach VOR and bears almost exactly on the 346-degree radial. So as you approach Meadowlark, plan to fly a FROM course on that radial from Seal Beach.

El Monte is roughly 14 nautical miles from the OMNI station, and its elevation is 296 feet. So plan your letdown and approach accordingly. You should be in visual contact slightly more than 10 miles from Seal Beach. And you'll soon see it's blue as promised.

El Monte's runway numbers are 19 and 1. So now on which end of the moonlit strip will you land, the near one or the far one?

What, you forgot the wind direction? Shame!

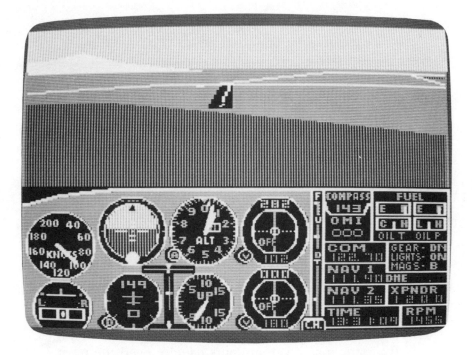

Touch and Go

North Position: 21377
East Position: 6617
Altitude: 1289
Pitch: 0
Bank: 0
Heading: 140
Airspeed: 112
Throttle: 19455

Rudder: 32767
Ailerons: 32767
Flaps: 0
Elevators: 32767 (IBM only)
Elevators: 36863 (all except IBM)
Time: 13:30
Season: 4—Fall
Wind: 8 Kts, 130

Here's a good setup for practicing landings—a picturesque final that needs you to add the touch of class.

You're approaching runway 15 at Renton Municipal, at the southern tip of Lake Washington. Renton is a city southeast of Seattle, population 30,612 before your arrival. Your approach is over Mercer Island, with Mount Rainier on the horizon.

You can make a normal landing, of course. Or you can practice *touch and go*, a popular training maneuver in which you make a flaps-down landing, and as soon as you're definitely on the ground, adjust elevator, flaps, power, and so on, and take off again, straight ahead. This obviates having to taxi back the length of the strip, wait your turn, and go through the whole takeoff procedure again. When you're renting an airplane, those are precious minutes. And since landing is the maneuver students usually need the most practice in, touch and go gets you more for your money.

Remember to use carburetor heat when you cut back your power on final. It prevents carburetor icing, which can cause engine failure. There's no reason not to leave the carb heat on all the way down. As old-time instructors say, "When in doubt, pull it out." (Carb heat is normally a push-pull control, which applies heat in the pulled-out position.)

Then, of course, remember that taking off the carb heat is part of getting ready to *go* after you *touch*, else you won't have full engine rpm (you'll hear and see the rpm drop when you apply heat and pick up when you remove it).

Remember to take off your flaps, too—and most important, to neutralize your elevators, which are probably almost all the way up when you touch down (or should be).

To add still more spice, or at least variety, to this landing, set a nighttime hour. Just go into edit mode and change the 13 to 23 before you fly the mode.

You have an alternative to making a landing, of course, if things don't look right—*going around*, that is, adding power, taking off flaps, and so forth, *before* you touch down, and then flying around the pattern to try another approach.

One last note: When you touch and go, the idea is to fly the pattern for as many takeoffs and landings as you feel like making. Or until your money runs out.

Strolling

North Position: 17083
East Position: 20993
Altitude: 17
Pitch: 0
Bank: 0
Heading: 45
Airspeed: 0
Throttle: 0

Rudder: 32767
Ailerons: 32767
Flaps: 0
Elevators: 32767
Time: 9:11
Season: 2—Spring
Wind: 4 Kts, 230

While you're looking straight ahead out your windshield, and without consulting any references, jot down a guess or so as to where you are.

The title gives you a clue. Here are a few others: You're somewhere in the area covered by your New York–Boston chart. You're on the ground, but you're not at an airport. You're not supposed to be where you are, even though it's a public place.

While you're guessing, look out anywhere *except* straight behind you. That's the *last* resort. Look out both sides, at all angles. Look down.

Then, when you give up or think you've guessed it, look behind you.

Sure enough.

 Now, before the police arrive on the scene, make an exit. Note that the wind is at your back, so perhaps you'd best turn around for your takeoff. Then, just take off normally. Grass makes a great strip. But watch out for bicyclists and other strollers.

Enjoy a little flight around the landmarks and then head for the nearest airport.

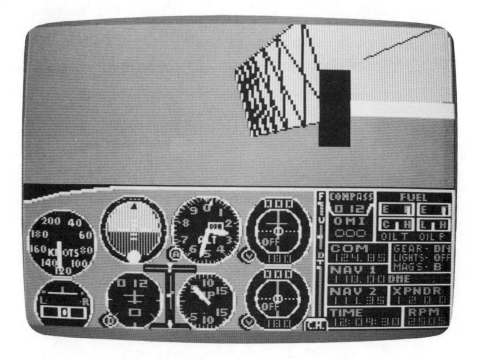

Yes or No?

North Position: 17194
East Position: 16663
Altitude: 2190 (IBM only)
Altitude: 2255 (all except IBM)
Pitch: 359
Bank: 0
Heading: 14 (IBM only)
Heading: 15 (all except IBM)
Airspeed: 142 (IBM only)
Airspeed: 121 (all except IBM)

Throttle: 32767 (IBM only)
Throttle: 22527 (all except IBM)
Rudder: 32767
Ailerons: 32767
Flaps: 0
Elevators: 29951 (IBM only)
Elevators: 36863 (all except IBM)
Time: 12:08
Season: 3—Summer
Wind: 0 Kts, 000

Don't touch the controls immediately. Instead, assess the situation. Decide if you *should* touch the controls.

Are you going to hit the John Hancock Building? Or are you going to fly safely over it?

Be sure the simulator has settled down and you have the true picture. Look at your instruments. Use your best judgment.

 If you think you'll fly safely over the top in the configuration you're in, don't touch anything. Except perhaps to set up a down view to see the building pass under you.

On the other hand, if you think you're going to hit the building, take corrective action before you get there.

Of course, unless you have super judgment, if you correct to save your skin, you'll never know whether you needed to, will you? And only one way to find out for sure, isn't there?

Ta-ta.

Of Sound Mind

North Position: 21526
East Position: 6666
Altitude: 603
Pitch: 0
Bank: 0
Heading: 180
Airspeed: 0
Throttle: 0

Rudder: 32767
Ailerons: 32767
Flaps: 0
Elevators: 32767
Time: 10:30
Season: 3— Summer
Wind: 4 Kts, 140

Runway 20 at Snohomish County Airport (Paine Field), Everett, Washington, is the smallest of the three strips. But plenty long enough to launch us on a nice sightseeing tour of one of the simulator's most scenic water areas—Puget Sound.

Before you taxi into position, tune your NAV to Paine VOR, 114.2, and set the OBI to the runway heading, 200, so we'll have a common distance reference. Your DME will read 0.6 nautical miles. (You'll readily see that there's a ten-degree error in the numbers for this runway on your simulator chart.)

Zoom out on radar until you see the Sound on your right and a highway far to the left. The highway is Interstate 5. We'll take off and fly straight on to the center of the Sound.

Now zoom in until you have good reference for the runway, just ahead of you.

Taxi out, get lined up heading 200, and take off as soon as you're ready. Climb straight out and level off at 2000.

When your DME reads 3.7, turn left to a heading of 170. You're now looking and flying down Puget Sound, toward Seattle center.

At about 5.5 miles, go into radar and zoom out until you see a second highway south, forking off from Interstate 5 to skirt the eastern side of Lake Washington (about eleven o'clock from your position). That highway is Interstate 405 to Bellevue and Renton. The land jutting out on the western side of the Sound is Point Jefferson, which is just slightly east of Port Madison Indian Reservation and a few miles from the grave of Chief Seattle of the Suquamish tribe.

If you take a right-front view at about 6.8 miles, you'll be looking directly into the body of water called Port Madison and toward the site of the Chief's grave on its banks.

A left front view will show you the northern area of Lake Washington and the network of highways serving Seattle.

At about 15 miles take another look out the left front and you'll see the Space Needle, which we encountered in an earlier chapter. That's at Seattle center. As it passes, look directly out the left side and you'll see two bridges crossing Lake Washington. The University of Washington is just north of the first one, and Seattle University just north of the second. The second bridge touches down on Mercer Island and continues as Interstate 90 all the way west to Spokane and beyond. The mountains in the background are part of the Cascade range, which stretches from top to bottom of the state, and includes Mount Rainier, which is about on the horizon.

The Cascade range confines most of the rain in the northwestern part of the state to the Puget Sound area, which is why this area is so green— and has so many waterways, bays, and islands.

When your DME reads about 21 miles, turn left ten degrees and head 160.

A few miles later, go into radar and adjust zoom until you see a point ahead of you where the Sound narrows and bends to the right. You'll be able to see this point out your windshield, now or shortly.

Aim your aircraft toward it.

What looks like an airport developing ahead of you is exactly that. And if you've flown other modes in this book, you've been there before: Tacoma Narrows. Remember the runway that reaches right out into the water?

However, Tacoma Narrows isn't our destination this time. Plan to fly around the point and out over the bay. When radar shows you're beyond the point, turn right to head approximately 222, or whatever course takes you toward the next narrow passage of water, with another bay beyond that. Radar will help you line up if you have trouble spotting it.

Now tune Olympia VORTAC on 113.4 and get a heading direct to Olympia Airport. You'll find you're approximately 16 to 19 miles out. Call the tower on 124.4 and find out which way they're landing. Chances are it's on runway 17. And you probably have the airport in sight.

Elevation at Olympia is 206 feet. A bit of judicious aileron work should get you lined up for a straight-in approach without much trouble. And you'll have seen all of Puget Sound in about 45 minutes.

Happy landings.

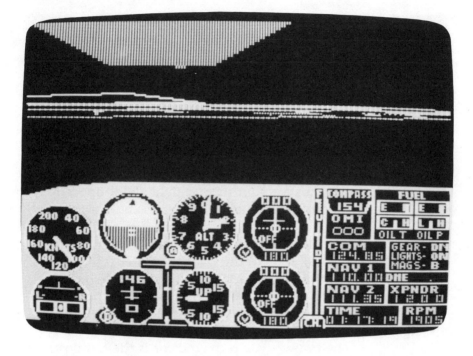

No Time to Be LAX

North Position: 15411
East Position: 5747
Altitude: 2000
Pitch: 0
Bank: 0
Heading: 150
Airspeed: 114
Throttle: 20479

Rudder: 32767
Ailerons: 32767
Flaps: 0
Elevators: 32767 (IBM only)
Elevators: 36863 (all except IBM)
Time: 1:15
Season: 3—Summer
Wind: 3 Kts, 60

You're over Santa Monica Bay in southern California, on base leg for runway 6L at Los Angeles International.

It's a beautiful night, and the view out your left side is a colorful one. You can pick out the runway at Santa Monica Municipal, and just south of that is Marina del Rey.

You'll want to get into approach configuration now, and start your turn to final about opposite the marina, because the runway is only a mile below the inlet. Your inbound heading will be 67 degrees (the runway is erroneously numbered). You're far enough out over the water (about seven or eight miles) to get lined up nice and straight. Elevation at LAX is 126. You can tune the VOR there on 113.6 if you like. And the tower frequency is 133.8.

The runway you're bound for is the leftmost straight line you'll see on final. It and its companion runway look like one wide strip, but they're not. A few miles off the end of the runway you'll see the lights around the marina. Then after the disk access, the runway gets outlined and all kinds of lights brighten your approach.

This mode is a good one to sharpen up your night perception and your approach precision. Get it down real fine and you might even want to try a nighttime touch and go.

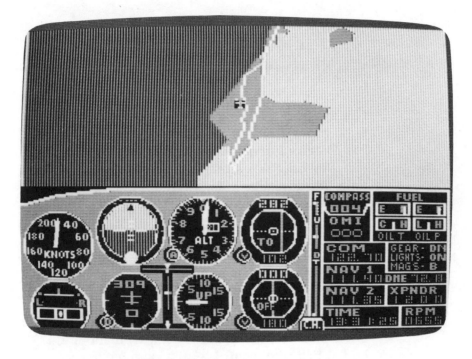

Fasten Seat Belts

North Position: 14758
East Position: 6106
Altitude: 15
Pitch: 0
Bank: 0
Heading: 9
Airspeed: 0
Throttle: 0

Rudder: 32767
Ailerons: 32767
Flaps: 0
Elevators: 32767
Time: 13:30
Season: 1—Winter
Wind 415 Kts, 300 (415 Kts =
   15 Kts + Turbulence Factor 4)*

*If turbulence is not implemented in your version of the simu-
lator, set wind to 4 Kts and ignore turbulence commentary.

Add for this mode:
Cloud Layer 2: Tops, 6000; Bottoms, 5000
Cloud Layer 1: Tops, 2000; Bottoms, 1500
Shear Zone Altitude 1: 3000

Not the best possible day for it, but you'll be making a trip up the southern coast of California, from San Diego's International Airport (Lindbergh Field) to Fallbrook Community Airpark, about 40 miles north. Fallbrook is a city (population 9000) just west of Interstate 15.

You're on the taxiway for runway 31. Go into radar and zoom until you can see the runway numbers ahead.

Call the tower on 134.8. They'll advise you of the ceiling. But not of the turbulence. You've heard other pilots reporting that. Anyway, it shouldn't be too bad (the factor is 4 of a possible 9).

Tune your NAV to Mission Bay VOR, 117.8, and set your OBI to intersect the 346-degree radial after you fly past the station, which will be a few minutes after you're airborne.

Zoom your radar out to a high altitude view so that you see Mission Bay behind your aircraft, together with most of the San Diego metropolitan area. Though it isn't featured in the simulation, there's a U.S. Naval Air Station across the bay on a little nub of land called North Island. And there's a Naval Training Center a few miles to your left. So watch out for navy jets.

The highway right off your nose is Interstate 5, and it's approximately paralleled by Interstate 805. Where they meet on the lower right of your screen is just about Tijuana, Mexico. (International, hmm?)

Continue taxiing, line up on the runway, and take off. Plan to cruise at 4500, between the cloud layers. And get on the 346 radial as soon as you have a FROM reading on your VOR indicator.

Wow! If this turbulence factor is 4, what's a 9? Thought this would be an easy flight, didn't you?

Fifty miles of this!? And weather on top of everything else. What in the world is so important that you just *have* to do at Fallbrook?

Will it ease off when we stop climbing?

Whatever you do, don't let that turbulence flip you over (it *can*).

Then, ah-h-h. Above 3000. Ah-h-h! Glass. A mere. Serenity. Bliss. So that's what shear altitude does. The wind and turbulence go from the surface to the shear zone altitude. Then both the wind and the turbulence quit. Lovely.

When your OBI indicates FROM, start flying to intersect the 346 radial. You were probably buffeted off your takeoff heading, and perhaps you're a bit disoriented. Remember, you can use the indicator to find out what radial you *are* on, if the needle is off the scale. Then you'll know which way to turn to intersect the radial you want. And ultimately, fly the needle (turn toward the needle). When the needle is centered, with your heading on the course selector, at that moment you're on the radial, so turn directly to the selected heading. You can, of course, anticipate it with a little practice. If you find, once you get on the radial, that the needle keeps moving to the left or right, correct your heading accordingly until it stays put. Just because your heading is 346 doesn't mean you'll stay on the 346 radial. Your nose could be pointed 330 or 360 or anywhere in between. You're only on the 346 radial if the OBI needle is centered on that heading. The culprit, of course, is the wind.

When you're settled down, at your altitude and on your heading, take a look at radar. You're pointed a bit inland. The metropolitan area ahead of you is Oceanside, California.

When your DME reads about 19.5 miles, adjust your radar to spot the city of Carlsbad's McClellan-Palomar runway to your left (nice how radar penetrates right through the overcast, isn't it?).

When you're 25 or 30 miles out from Mission Bay VOR, you might as well face the fact that you have to let down and make a landing in all that turbulence. Because, of course, the turbulence didn't go away below you. Where would it go?

Fallbrook's elevation is 708 feet, and the runway you're supposed to land on is 36.

As you descend through the overcast, your instruments are all you have. So don't even consider the possibility that they're wrong. At such times, they're right even if they're wrong, because your instincts are worse than the worst instruments. In fact, in this stuff there's no such thing as instinct. Or seat of the pants, either. Just look at that artificial horizon dance!

The ground comes into view at 1500. So try to stay on (or get back to) that heading of 346.

Won't you be glad when this turkey's on the ground? Anywhere on the ground!

If you happen to see a black (orange on the IBM) mountain, the runway's somewhere this side of it. By the same token, if you happen to see a runway, there's a black mountain somewhere the other side of it.

If you land even close to the runway at Fallbrook, you can be very proud of yourself.

And it you don't, so what? Who ever heard of a black (or orange) mountain anyway?

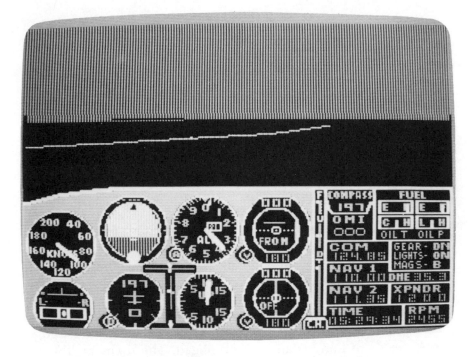

Making Tracks

North Position: 17642
East Position: 21351
Altitude: 174
Pitch: 0
Bank: 0
Heading: 180
Airspeed: 0
Throttle: 0

Rudder: 32767
Ailerons: 32767
Flaps: 0
Elevators: 32767
Time: 5:25
Season: 3—Summer
Wind: 7 Kts, 165

Daylight is still a few minutes away as you prepare to depart runway 19 at Bradley International, Windsor Locks, Connecticut.

You're out early because you're going on a long trip—not in terms of flying time, but of time itself. In a sense, you're going to fly back through it. Also, it's a Saturday, and you don't want to waste any of your precious weekend.

 Tune your NAV to Madison VOR, 110.4, and set the course selector to 196 before your departure.

 Take off when you're set, and climb out on the 190-degree runway heading. As you pass through 1000, turn slightly right to exactly 196. Level off at 2500.

When you have the altitude and daylight, switch on radar and zoom out until you see a little wedge of Long Island Sound ahead. The highway, the only one you see, is Interstate 91.

Back to your out-the-windshield view, the airport ahead, just east of I-91, is Hartford-Brainard. And now you can see Long Island Sound, even though it's some 30 miles away.

Take a look behind at the airport you just left.

As Hartford-Brainard disappears off your windshield, you might want to go into radar and zoom in until the runways appear, looking like a railroad signal or half a pole-vaulting rig. Then return to your out-the-windshield view.

 Now, be sure to include the DME regularly in your instrument scan. When it reads 21 miles, take a ground view, looking directly down past your wheel, and poise your finger over the Pause key. When the reading is 20.4, press the key.

Why are we looking down at this particular patch of green? There is absolutely nothing to distinguish it from thousands of miles of green elsewhere in the simulator (and the world). At least, nothing we can see.

But look harder. You're just south of a town named Rocky Hill. And there used to be a river where you're gazing. About a mile to the left of this point is what's left of the river, now called the Connecticut River (it doesn't appear in the simulation).

The river began to dry up awhile ago—two hundred million years ago to be inexact. And the area you're looking down at became very muddy.

So muddy that the dinosaurs who strode the earth at that time left their tracks in the mud. And the tracks became embedded in the earth's crust, more or less permanently (fossilized). There are hundreds of such dinosaur footprints down there below you, a bit south of Rocky Hill, Connecticut. And that's why they've named the area Dinosaur State Park. If you can't see the footprints from where you are, perhaps you're just not looking hard enough.

 Time now for breakfast. Why not make a slight turn right to a heading of 210? It'll take you straight to Tweed–New Haven Airport in a matter of minutes. They'll be landing on runway 20, elevation 13 feet. Or if you're starving, that's Meriden Markham Municipal you see a little ahead across the highway.

Then when you've had your bacon and a couple of dinosaur eggs over light, you can make tracks again.

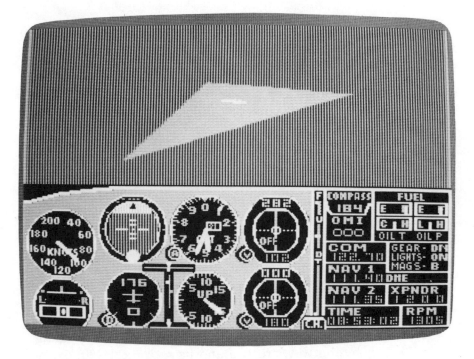

Space Glide

North Position: 17404
East Position: 21723
Altitude: 14750
Pitch: 0
Bank: 0
Heading: 173
Airspeed: 125
Throttle: 0

Rudder: 32767
Ailerons: 32767
Flaps: 0
Elevators: 45567 (IBM only)
Elevators: 40447 (all except IBM)
Time: 8:52
Season: 2—Spring
Wind: 0 Kts, 000

Throttle may not be used in this mode.

Imagine you're in a space shuttle returning from many days in orbit. You have reentered the atmosphere and must set up your glide to land on the runway you see on the little island directly off your nose. You may land from either direction, since there is no wind. But if you miss the runway, your gear will collapse in soft ground, and you will probably destroy your high-technology, multi-million-dollar spacecraft. Or worse.

 Take over as soon as you exit edit mode and give it your best shot. What the astronauts do is circle the landing target as they lose altitude. That seems like a reasonable procedure, but you may think of some other approach.

Whatever you do, it's a good idea to keep the island in view as you glide. The runway headings, by the way, are 100 and its reciprocal 280, or numbers 10 and 28. Field elevation is 105 feet and the runway is 2500 feet long. That's *much* shorter than the deluxe freeways the astronauts land on.

So drive carefully. And if you set her down on the runway, then, as the saying goes, "Outstanding!"
Good luck.

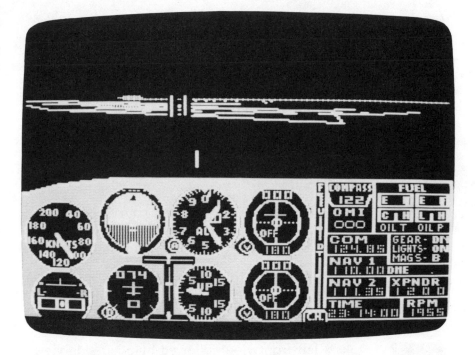

Central Issue

North Position: 17027
East Position: 20942
Altitude: 1000
Pitch: 359
Bank: 0
Heading: 76
Airspeed: 112 (IBM only)
Airspeed: 120 (all except IBM)
Throttle: 21503 (IBM only)

Throttle: 19455 (all except IBM)
Rudder: 32767
Ailerons: 32767
Flaps: 0
Elevators: 32767 (IBM only)
Elevators: 36863 (all except IBM)
Time: 23:11
Season: 3—Summer
Wind: 5 Kts, 70

You're over Jersey City, New Jersey, pointed across Upper Bay of the Hudson River and toward the Statue of Liberty as well as the lower tip of Manhattan. The city is a festival of light in the distance, as you'd expect.

Continue on course, adjusting pitch or power if necessary to maintain your thousand feet of altitude.

Beyond the statue are the familiar World Trade Center towers.

After the disk access, try to aim your aircraft so the statue will pass directly under you (you'll have to be pretty quick), and take a momentary down view.

Next, head the plane so you'll pass just to the right of the Trade Center towers (there'll be another disk access as you fly).

Take a left-front view followed by a left-side view to get a dramatic close-up of the buildings as they go by.

Now turn left and set up a course to the left of the Empire State Building. Central Park, 26 blocks north of that landmark, will look like a huge green or orange runway ahead of you.

And who could resist such a beautiful grass strip? Plus the fact that—compliments of the simulator—there are no gulleys, lakes, trees, roads, or other natural paraphernalia of the real Central Park to contend with on this flight.

So I don't have to tell you what to do, do I? (Elevation is 20 feet.)

But be sure to enjoy some close-ups of the grand old Empire State Building on the way.

After you've looked around, tune your NAV to Carmel VOR, 116.6, and center the OBI needle with a TO indication. Then take off, climb to 2000, and fly the needle. Be sure to look behind you as you climb out. Pretty.

You're headed for a real (genuine, serious) landing at Westchester County Airport, about 12 miles this side of the OMNI station you've tuned.

By the time you have your altitude, things look pretty dark ahead, don't they? Even those highway lights on the right of your windshield begin to slip away. And around 26 miles out, they're gone.

Dark, isn't it? Kind of time when you look somewhere other than straight ahead just to see some light.

But, then, aha! Some neat blue lights ahead. Civilization.

Radar doesn't provide any clue as to what the blue lights are, but they persist. Perhaps they're the Westchester County runway lights?

The closer we get, the more it looks like those are runways, for sure. Westchester has three strips. (If you're flying an Archer, you never had the least doubt, did you?) There's no tower in the simulator for this airport, but assuming the winds haven't shifted, our runway of choice is 6. Elevation of the airport is 439 feet.

When you're convinced that you have your runway in view, figure they're flying a righthand pattern. Base leg is 330 degrees.

After you land, a cup of coffee would be great, wouldn't it? But you're lucky if you find anything open in the airport at this hour. If you do, play it cool. Have your coffee. But don't go bragging about how you landed in Central Park en route.

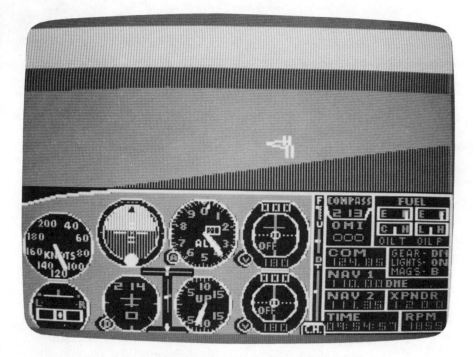

Have a Nuys
Day

North Position: 15503
East Position: 5813
Altitude: 799
Pitch: 0
Bank: 0
Heading: 161
Airspeed: 0
Throttle: 0

Add for this mode:
Reliability Factor, 50

Rudder: 32767
Ailerons: 32767
Flaps: 0
Elevators: 32767
Time: 9:15
Season: 3—Summer
Wind: 4 Kts, 170

If you're like me, you wondered about that "reliability factor" thing for a while before you decided to try it. You were busy enough just learning how to taxi the airplane reasonably, and then fly and land it well.

Then, there was finding out what clouds were like in the simulator, and next (as earlier in this book) exploring turbulence.

Reliability, on the other hand, is a biggie.

What happens when reliability is cut to, say, 50 percent, as in this present mode?

I don't really know. So let's find out together. I'll tell you what happens to me on this nice morning—cloudless, light wind, no special problems other than reliability. And you see what happens to you.

Let's assume we're just going to fly contact in a relatively familiar area (familiar, that is, if you've flown several other Los Angeles area modes in this book). We're nicely positioned for runway 16 at Van Nuys Airport in California. So let's plan to take off and fly toward the coast, then down it, at about 2500 feet, just sightseeing (and reliability watching).

 First of all, if ever you checked controls this is the time for it. See if you have right and left aileron, and elevator and flaps, and that they operate in the right direction.

I have right and left aileron, and elevator and flaps, and they operate in the right direction (according, at least, to my instrument panel).

I'm also checking carburetor heat on/off—okay. Altimeter—reasonable reading. Directional gyro—agrees with compass. Fuel—okay. Oil temp—okay. Oil pressure—okay.

Next, with brakes held on, I run the engine up to maximum rpm, even though the brakes won't quite hold the airplane. Looks okay.

Tune Santa Monica VOR 110.8, just to check the set. Shows 13-odd miles. Looks okay.

 So there's nothing left to do but get this turkey into the air and see what happens. Come on and take off and fly with me.

 At a thousand feet I turn right ten degrees to point toward the ocean. Everything seems normal. Maybe a 50 percent reliability factor means a 50 percent dependability factor, muse I. There's as much chance that everything will function okay as that something will go ape?

Now I sit here and start reasoning with myself. I figure whatever is in store for this airplane, it won't have to do with the mechanical controls, ailerons, elevator, flaps. The controls won't suddenly reverse if they weren't reversed on the ground. And unless there's a giant fuel leak, I'm not suddenly going to run out of gas. My throttle's functioning normally. Oil gauges still look good.

So the most likely failure will be some kind of engine failure.

And if I stay near the coast, there are plenty of airports should I have to make a forced landing—seven of them, in fact.

This may turn out to be a dull morning (from a reliability standpoint, I mean). I begin wondering what 20 percent reliability would be like. Or maybe zero reliability.

Fifty-fifty odds are, after all, pretty good odds. Say, you had a fifty-fifty chance to win a million dollars.

I do my instrument scan far more religiously than usual. I even look out at my wing tips to see if maybe one's tearing loose.

Ridiculous.

Since I'm flying Cessna, in a fit of bravado I raise my gear, though I usually fly with it down.

(I fantasize a Cessna 150 when I fly the Microsoft simulator, since that's the airplane I learned in. And it certainly didn't have retractable gear.) I figure maybe the gear won't lower. But I toggle the G key, and sure enough the gear is operating fine.

I try to remember, should my engine quit, what keys switch magnetos. It's somewhere in the manual, but I can't remember thing one about them. So I just keep flying, fat, dumb, and happy.

 When I reach the coast I turn left to head 145. And keep flying. Looking frequently out the left side to check out the various airports along the way.

At 9:39:05 even the clock's working.

But I'm fresh out of airports for awhile, at least right on the coast. As I go by LA International, Torrance is the next good possibility. I'm more or less on a heading for that airport, I figure.

I begin wondering whether the reliability is randomized. Whether 50 percent on one flight gives you X possible failures and on another flight, Y possibles. Along with Z probabilities of their happening or not happening, based purely on a roll of the dice.

My estimate that I was on an approximate heading for Torrance was wrong. A chance look out the left side shows me Torrance farther inland than I thought.

I start toying with the idea of hopping over to Catalina, feeling more secure with this 50 percent airplane all the time.

 So I tune Santa Catalina VOR on 111.4 and look at the DME. About 27 miles.

Are you game? (Or did you land with an engine out somewhere behind me? Or did you never get off the Van Nuys runway?)

If you're with me, get an OBI course and fly it. We'll see what's happenin' on Catalina Island.

The course I read out is 164. Yours may be different.

I'm on my way.

Everything seems to be A-OK—airspeed, altimeter, fuel, oil, straight-and-level at 2500.

I begin to think maybe I'll go into edit mode for a second, and check to make sure the reliability factor is still 50 and didn't sneak back to 100. And at the same moment I'm thinking that, I get a disk access. So I decide to wait a few minutes and see if the new overlay has any problems in it.

At the moment, the clock reads 9:45:23, and I'm 21 miles from Santa Catalina OMNI. All the gauges look right and the engine's still humming. The sky's still blue.

At 9:48:50, I go into edit mode and check the reliability factor. Just before I do, Catalina runway gets visible ahead.

Reliability factor reads 50.

I resume the flight.

At 10.5 miles out of Catalina, I decide to turn left to a heading of 130, as a base leg for Catalina's runway 22, and then get on a long final—really long—just for kicks.

I remind myself that the elevation of the airport on the island is way up there, 1602 feet. So I decide I'm already at an acceptable pattern altitude.

I make my right turn and see by the DME I'm on a 4.5 mile final. And my altitude is 2200.

I wonder whether you're still with me.

I see-saw around a bit trying to get lined up well, and I make a pretty hard landing. But I'm on the ground.

This compromised airplane got me into the air, took me down the coast over Santa Monica Bay, then flew me all the way across the Gulf of Santa Catalina.

I call her "Ol' Reliable."

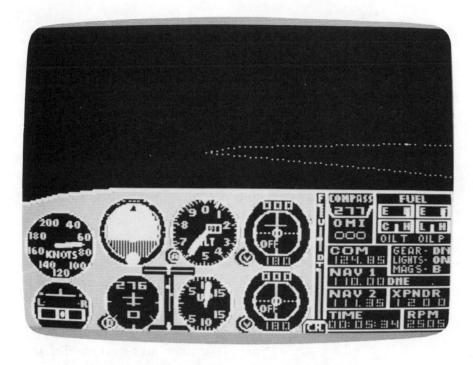

Twilight Zone

North Position: 17100
East Position: 16931
Altitude: 591
Pitch: 0
Bank: 0
Heading: 250
Airspeed: 0
Throttle: 0

Rudder: 32767
Ailerons: 32767
Flaps: 0
Elevators: 32767
Time: 0:00
Season: 2—Spring
Wind: 10 Kts, 300

Do not precede this mode with another night flight mode.

Sorry to disappoint Archer pilots, but the twilight zone exists only in the Microsoft world. But go ahead and read, and then fly out with the Cessna pilot, if you don't mind taking off in pitch darkness.

Surely, this is a grass strip somewhere, because you're in your airplane and ready to take off. If not for the fact that there's no runway as such, everything seems normal.

Or does it? Look at the clock.
A few seconds after midnight.
If it's midnight, then where's the darkness? And if there's no darkness, is it daytime? Is the clock wrong? Or are we on the other side of the Arctic night? Or what?
That sky so blue. That grass so green. And that hour so late. Zero hour. Witches and spells. Midnight. In a world—where?

Should your lights be on or off? Toggle them, and see if it makes any difference. Do lights a nighttime make?
Weird.

Take a look off your right wing tip.
Weirder yet. Since when was your airplane black?
Take a look behind you. Tail, too. Jet black.
If it weren't for the fact that there's daylight all around you, this could be scary. No matter what view you take, there's the daylight. You're sitting in the middle of daytime. But at midnight.
A mystic might venture a guess that *you* are the night. You and your plane. You've reversed roles with the darkness. You are *the pilot of darkness.*

And your plane is *the aircraft of darkness.*

Let's get out of here. Take off. Straight ahead.
Let's see if we can fly out of this insanity.

That monotonous green horizon drops under
our nose. And that sky is a notorious blue. It
continues blue. And it's only minutes past
midnight.

Did the takeoff seem a little slow to you? It did
to me. Everything seems a little slow in this
strange place.

Maybe climb on out until we can see something,
anything, ahead.

Climbing to 500...2000. The horizon now seems to
stay put. Only a look out the side tells us we're
climbing normally. If anything lofted on that omi-
nous black wing could be said to be normal.

To 2500...3000. Still no landmarks. Anywhere.

Now at 3500...4000. No. Nothing but daylight.
Daylight at midnight. Weird.

Try radar. Zoom out three, six, a dozen notches.
What do you see?

Where are the landmarks? Where on Earth is
Earth?

Start planning to level off at 6000.

But perhaps even before you reach 6000 or perhaps by the time you read this or slightly after,
something will happen. That familiar whirring
sound. Sort of like strange wings. Maybe flying
you into something. Or out of something. Read no
further until it does.

Now time has caught up with you (or you've
caught up with it) and things are normal again—
at least for the hour you're flying into (or out of).

Turn toward those lights at the right of your windshield. To a heading of, say, 270 or 275, so the two rows of lights come together at center screen. And do what's necessary to get an altimeter reading of 6000.

Note, as you do, that there's a blinking light just to the right of that little island of orange dots. That must mean an airport, mustn't it?

Point your aircraft toward the beacon. There'll be still another beacon to the right of that one. In fact, two of them, one slightly above the other.

Go into radar and zoom in or out until you see the beacon flashing (on radar) ahead of you. That shape you're flying on the edge of look a little familiar?

Just keep pointed toward that leftmost beacon. And start a gradual descent to 3000. You've a distance to go.

While you're flying, you might try to figure out where you've come from. Somewhere where night was daytime and your beautiful plane was painted anthracite.

Let's just say it was somewhere not on your charts. Like a different state.

Or a different State.

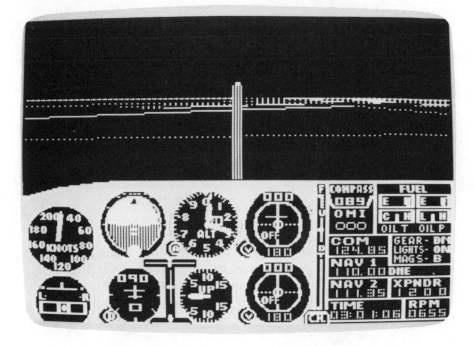

Olympic Run

North Position: 21740
East Position: 6375
Altitude: 289
Pitch: 0
Bank: 0
Heading: 90
Airspeed: 0
Throttle: 0

Rudder: 32767
Ailerons: 32767
Flaps: 0
Elevators: 32767
Time: 5:00
Season: 3—Summer
Wind: 6 Kts, 220

Add for this mode:
Wind Level 1: Knots, 210; Degrees, 280
Shear Zone Altitude 1: 4000

If turbulence is not implemented in your version of the simulator, set wind to 10 Kts and ignore turbulence commentary.

Dawn on William R. Fairchild International Airport, Port Angeles, Washington, finds you pointed down the taxiway for runway 26. Your position and the airport lighting conditions give you a good chance to practice visual taxiing (without reference to radar). The setup is very realistic. Try following the lights on the taxiway down to the far end of the runway, making your turn and getting lined up.

Start off and steer a bit to the left, using the blue lights as your guide. Stay between the lights, paralleling the runway, and at the far end make a sharp left turn onto the centerline, which is also blue in the simulation. The actual runway heading is 267.

If you call the tower on 122.8, you'll "hear" a slightly sleepy voice tell you that the active runway is 25. No such animal.

Before you take off, tune Tatoosh OMNI on 112.2, and center the needle to fly to the station. You'll see your initial heading will be 262 degrees, and the distance is about 47 miles.

Go ahead and get airborne, making a slight left turn to your heading as you climb out. Be sure to take a glance behind you, noting the airport outlines and—the green area in the distance—the city of Port Angeles.

For the present, plan on a cruising altitude of 3500 feet (we'll experiment above this altitude a little later on).

You're flying approximately west along the northern coast of the state of Washington, toward the northwesternmost tip of the United States.

The Strait of Juan de Fuca, an inlet of the Pacific, is on your right, and across the strait is British Columbia (you have a private grass strip over there, remember?).

Take a look out the left side. Though you can't see it, there's a giant area off your wing tip called Olympic National Park. It is one of the nation's most scenic, with rain forests, lush vegetation, skyscraper-high spruce and fir trees, and many mountains including a Mount Olympus which rivals that of Greece, dwelling place of the deities.

Stay on the 262-degree radial.

At 5:30 daylight will turn on.

Our intent is to fly to the northwestern tip of the Olympic Peninsula, which is all that area between the Pacific Ocean and Puget Sound. At daylight you'll see the Pacific ahead of you.

If you look at Tatoosh on your Seattle area chart, you'll see that the 262-degree radial is pointing you south of the tip. But to pinpoint the tip (it's called Cape Flattery) exactly, we can fly the 290-degree radial FROM Tatoosh. And that's what we plan to do.

Thus, when you're over Tatoosh (DME reads 0), turn right to a 290-degree heading. And when the OBI settles down, track the needle on the 290 radial.

For all practical purposes, when your DME shows you're ten miles from the VOR, you're over the Pacific off Cape Flattery, as far northwest as you can fly in the United States. The geography of the simulator isn't at all sharp as regards this landmark, but anyway you did it.

So now turn left to head approximately 150, and you'll find you're flying down the western edge of the peninsula. Tune your NAV to Hoquiam, 117.7, and keep flying until the station comes into range. Your chart will show you that you're heading in approximately the right direction. You can set the OBI to 150 in anticipation of the station getting active, which it will when your DME starts reading.

Meanwhile, we promised a little experiment above your cruising altitude, and this is a good time for it.

Remember that we set a turbulence factor of 2 for this mode, with our 210 knots at wind level 1. The turbulence factor is multiplied by 100, and the wind (10 knots at 280) is added to that. We set the shear zone altitude at 4000.

So let's climb through 4000 now to, say, 4500 and see what a turbulence factor of 2 gives us in the way of instability. Use a rate-of-climb of 1000 feet per minute.

Note the turbulence about midway between 4000 and 4500. The airplane just doesn't want to hold that heading, does it? But keep fighting it.

Or should you fight it?

Let's try another experiment.

Lose some altitude again until you get out of the clear air turbulence. Then reestablish your 150-degree heading and climb back up into the turbulence to 4500 feet.

This time don't fight the controls; don't use aileron. Let's see whether the heading averages out in the turbulent air.

Your DME is already, or soon will be, active. It turns on between 69 and 70 miles out.

Well, the heading sure doesn't average out, does it? Very quickly you're way off course.

Descend below the turbulence again (you've plenty of time—it's a long way to Hoquiam). Set your OBI to fly the 140-degree radial to the station. Then do what you have to do to get on that radial. If you're a fledgling at this, remember that you're on the radial indicated by the OBI when the needle is centered, no matter what heading you may be on. If, in relatively still air, you then turn direct to the heading indicated by the OBI, your compass, directional gyro, and OBI setting are, or soon will be, all in agreement. Then, depending on the wind direction and velocity, your aircraft may head off the radial. So make whatever corrections are needed to keep the needle centered. When it's centered, you're on the desired radial regardless of what compass heading your nose may be following.

Once you're settled on course, straight and level at 3500, and clearly on the 140-degree radial with the OBI active, climb back up to 4500 at about 500 feet per minute. Remember to level off at your altitude—don't let the turbulence mess you up.

Now fly the OBI needle as well as the directional gyro and compass. Follow the needle; if the needle is to the right of center, use aileron to correct to the right, and vice versa if the needle is left of center. You're always flying toward the needle, trying to keep it centered (without departing so far from your essential heading that you're on the reciprocal).

Since the radial you're on (in this case 140) represents a straight line through the air (and toward the station), your gyro or compass heading assumes less importance. You may be flying sideways, but your path through the air is relatively straight.

Trying to keep your wings level (in the simulator turbulence, at least) requires undue effort and just adds to the confusion. The simulator doesn't really bounce you up and down, as does actual turbulence. It simulates this with wing wagging. Note that there are no significant changes in your rate-of-climb indication, and your altitude remains quite stable.

 Looking from the airplane to the left or right side gives you a more realistic *feel* of turbulence than does looking straight ahead. The wing wagging then looks more like abrupt altitude changes, as the side horizon pops up and down.

 Stay in the turbulence as long as you like. Personally, I find it the least realistic aspect of the simulator, and a factor of 1 is usually plenty if I feel I want any turbulence at all.

When you've had enough bobbing around, descend to your cruising altitude of 3500 and get clearly back on the 140-degree radial until you're about 30 miles from the Hoquiam VOR. Then turn left to a heading of 90 degrees and tune your NAV to Olympia VORTAC, 113.4. Your DME will show you you're some 60 to 65 miles from that station. Set your OBI and make any corrections necessary to fly the 90-degree radial inbound for Olympia Airport.

The highway you see ahead is U.S. 101, which skirts the whole peninsula.

See if you can raise the Olympia control tower on 124.4. If not, just wait. They may contact you after the disk access; otherwise, contact them. They'll probably advise they're landing on runway 26 since the wind is from 220.

 Elevation at Olympia is 206 feet. As you get closer in, plan a real professional approach, entering the downwind leg (80 degrees) at a 45-degree angle (35-degree heading). After your superb landing, you'll be just in time for breakfast.

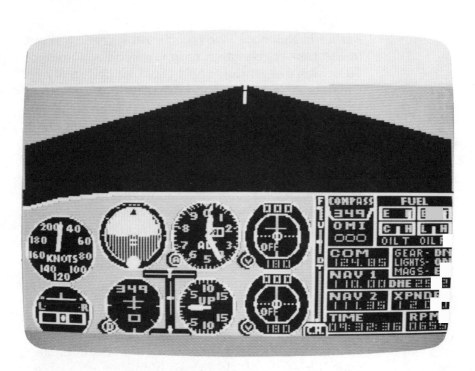

If...Then... Else

North Position: 17402
East Position: 21435
Altitude: 416
Pitch: 0
Bank: 0
Heading: 55
Airspeed: 0
Throttle: 0

Add for this mode:
Reliability Factor, 10

Rudder: 32767
Ailerons: 32767
Flaps: 0
Elevators: 32767
Time: 9:30
Season: 3—Summer
Wind: 8 Kts, 000

Earlier in this book, we (or at least I) made a flight in the Los Angeles area with a reliability setting of 50. It was uneventful, and I (we?) landed safely on Catalina Island. As I said at that time, I wondered whether you were with me, or perhaps never got off the runway or made a forced landing somewhere.

Anyway, our experiments (or mine anyway) would be incomplete without trying a decidedly lower reliability. If this flight is uneventful—at least from a reliability standpoint (no flight is uneventful from a flying standpoint)—then we'll have learned that the reliability factor needn't be regarded too seriously.

The prior sentence, like a well-known command in the BASIC language, has an IF and a THEN. It can also have an ELSE. IF such and such is true, THEN do so and so, ELSE do so and so.

And so here we are at Chester Airport, Chester, Connecticut, all fired up in a highly questionable crate. Or, so to speak, in two highly questionable crates—yours and mine. We might as well fly together, in some kind of compromised formation, like a pair of barnstormers in the early days, never knowing when the engine will sputter and quit, we'll spring an oil leak, some fabric will tear off a wing, or whatever. Yours or mine.

If we can get off the ground, let's hop across Long Island Sound to Long Island MacArthur Airport. (Douglas "Old Soldiers Never Die" MacArthur would be proud of us.)

 I won't spell out the preflight checks you should make. I'll be too busy making my own. But I'll tell you when I'm ready to take off (runway 35) and what happens thereafter.

(Long pause.)

I'm ready to take off. I'm taking off. Follow me-e-e-e-e!

I'm climbing through 1000 and making a climbing turn left to a heading of 240, just for starters.

Heading 240 at 2000, I'm tuning Deer Park VOR on 111.2. DME reads 48.8 miles. Before I adjust the OBI for a reading, I level off at 2500.

I center the OBI needle and get a reading of 240 (how's that for eyeballing it!).

Disk access.

Where are you? Are you with me?

Crate's great to date.

Long Island Sound's nice and blue ahead.

Forty-three miles to go. Just possibly this reliability thing is purely in the imagination. We're supposed to imagine it, I mean. It isn't for real.

Let's see, reliability of 10 on a scale of 100 means nine chances in ten that things'll go—not right—but wrong! Or is it right? My math was never very good. (But I recall reading that Einstein, too, had trouble with simple arithmetic. Minds like his and mine are concerned with more profound things.)

Are you flying? Are you still there?

Forty miles to go.

Thirty-eight miles to go. Take a look out the right side and there's Tweed–New Haven Airport. Wonder if they fixed the pothole yet.

Straight-and-level at 2500. Indicating about 108. Thirty-three and a half miles to go.

Would you set out to cross a desert in a 10 percent reliable car?

Thirty miles to go. Needle a couple of degrees off. Have to correct right a bit.

Lot of water down there. At 28 miles out, radar says I'm about in the middle of it.

Maybe they accidentally left the reliability factor out of my disk. A slight oversight. An infinitesimal flaw. Maybe they abandoned the idea and forgot to delete it from the manual.

Twenty-five miles to go.

Maybe I'm being too conservative. Maybe I should get a little altitude and try a loop or a barrel roll. (Just kidding.)

What are you doing? Are you with me? Are you reading this in a ditch somewhere? Or in the middle of an expressway?

Twenty-three miles.

Twenty miles.

9:50.

What's your clock say?

Seventeen miles. I'm just about over land now. Need still more correction to the right.

Fourteen point six miles. And I think that's MacArthur ahead. It's a little left of the OMNI anyway.

Elevation at the General's is 99 feet. No tower there. But considering the wind, I should land to the east. Runway heading looks like 70 degrees. So I'll fly out over the ocean and do a 180.

Still about six miles from the airport, I guess. I'll pass a bit to the left of it to allow for my turn.

Are you still there? Do you believe this reliability thing? I'm beginning to have my doubts. Really, 10 percent reliability ought to be more exciting than this. Maybe we should have set 1 percent?

Airport's passing to my right now. Heading out over the ocean. Never heard an engine purr so pretty. Never flew straighter and leveler. Never saw everything work so perfectly. They could even use this clock to set Greenwich mean time.

Just looked down, and I'm over the water. Time
to start my 180. Are you there? Are you with me?

Beautiful, controlled two-minute turn. Masterful.
What a beautiful day for flyin'.

Back off on the power. Runway not in sight yet.
Passing through 330 degrees. Now I see it.

I'm way too far left. Didn't plan that too well.
Have to get over there and get lined up right.

Heading 44 now and that can't be runway 7,
and I can't tell which one *is*.

Trying radar. Can't raise the airport at all on
there. Have no time, anyway. Back to out the
windshield.

Should I go around? Altitude 1200 feet. Might
as well land on that runway whatever number it
is. Artwick will never know.

Yes, get in position and take it. Approach is
lousy, sloppy, miserable.

Now left. Not too steep. Straighten it out. You'll
land across it if you don't. Too much altitude.
How far am I? Take it easy. You've got her. Coming up fine. Now your left turn. No. Straighten
out. Got to go more right then left. Hope nobody's
watching. Now left. Forget flaps. More left. Coming up now. Six hundred feet. Descending 500.
Hope nobody's watching. All the power off.
Overcontrolling. Too low. Down too fast—1500
feet a minute. Ridiculous. Add power. Get over to
the right. Bank's too steep. That squeal. Runway.

And all that glass. All that beautiful glass.
Shattered.

Where are you? I don't see you. Did you make
it? Did you ever take off?

At any rate, when I see you, I'll give you the
lowdown on this reliability thing. I figured it all
out. It's like this: When you enter a reliability factor of 10, everything works fine. The engine purrs.
The clock keeps time. The gear goes up and

down. The lights go on and off. The ailerons aren't crossed. The elevator functions fine. The OMNI is right on. The grass is green. The sky is blue. The airplane flies like a dream. Everything's perfect. Except for one thing:

The bank's too steep.

Just a last word to clear up any misconceptions you may have from this book concerning the Reliability Factor. Since we had Reality set to 0 for all the adventures, the Reliability always stayed at 100 regardless of the percentage we entered. Set the Reality to 1 and the Reliability to 10 and see what happens.

So long. Thanks for your company. Happy flying.

COMPUTE! Books

Ask your retailer for these **COMPUTE! Books** or order directly from **COMPUTE!**.

Call toll free (in US) **800-334-0868** (in NC 919-275-9809) or write COMPUTE! Books, P.O. Box 5058, Greensboro, NC 27403.

Quantity	Title	Price*	Total
_____	Machine Language for Beginners (11-6)	**$14.95**	_____
_____	The Second Book of Machine Language (53-1)	**$14.95**	_____
_____	COMPUTE!'s Guide to Adventure Games (67-1)	**$12.95**	_____
_____	Computing Together: A Parents & Teachers Guide to Computing with Young Children (51-5)	**$12.95**	_____
_____	Personal Telecomputing (47-7)	**$12.95**	_____
_____	BASIC Programs for Small Computers (38-8)	**$12.95**	_____
_____	Programmer's Reference Guide to the Color Computer (19-1)	**$12.95**	_____
_____	Home Energy Applications (10-8)	**$14.95**	_____
	The Home Computer Wars: An Insider's Account of Commodore and Jack Tramiel		
_____	Hardback (75-2)	**$16.95**	_____
_____	Paperback (78-7)	**$ 9.95**	_____
_____	The Book of BASIC (61-2)	**$12.95**	_____
_____	Every Kid's First Book of Robots and Computers (05-1)	**$ 4.95†**	_____
_____	The Beginner's Guide to Buying a Personal Computer (22-1)	**$ 3.95†**	_____
_____	The Greatest Games: The 93 Best Computer Games of all Time (95-7)	**$ 9.95**	_____
_____	Investment Management with Your Personal Computer (005)	**$14.95**	_____
_____	40 Great Flight Simulator Adventures (022-X)	**$ 9.95**	_____

* Add $2.00 per book for shipping and handling.
† Add $1.00 per book for shipping and handling.
Outside US add $5.00 air mail or $2.00 surface mail.

NC residents add 4.5% sales tax. _____
Shipping & handling: $2.00/book _____
Total payment _____

All orders must be prepaid (check, charge, or money order).
All payments must be in US funds.
☐ Payment enclosed.
Charge ☐ Visa ☐ MasterCard ☐ American Express

Acct. No. _____ Exp. Date _____
                                                                    (Required)
Name _____

Address _____

City _____ State _____ Zip _____

*Allow 4–5 weeks for delivery.
Prices and availability subject to change.
Current catalog available upon request.

If you've enjoyed the articles in this book, you'll find the same style and quality in every monthly issue of **COMPUTE!** Magazine. Use this form to order your subscription to **COMPUTE!**.

For Fastest Service
Call Our **Toll-Free** US Order Line
800-334-0868
In NC call 919-275-9809

COMPUTE!
P.O. Box 5058
Greensboro, NC 27403

My computer is:
☐ Commodore 64 ☐ TI-99/4A ☐ IBM PC or PCjr ☐ VIC-20 ☐ PET
☐ Radio Shack Color Computer ☐ Apple ☐ Atari ☐ Other _____
☐ Don't yet have one...

☐ $24 One Year US Subscription
☐ $45 Two Year US Subscription
☐ $65 Three Year US Subscription
Subscription rates outside the US:

☐ $30 Canada and Foreign Surface Mail
☐ $65 Foreign Air Delivery

Name _____

Address _____

City _____ State _____ Zip _____

Country _____

Payment must be in US funds drawn on a US bank, international money order, or charge card.
☐ Payment Enclosed   ☐ Visa
☐ MasterCard   ☐ American Express

Acct. No. _____ Expires _____ / _____
                                              (Required)

Your subscription will begin with the next available issue. Please allow 4–6 weeks for delivery of first issue. Subscription prices subject to change at any time.

759199

Notes

Notes